Whispers from the Maple on the Hill

Whispers from the Maple on the Hill

Life During the Depression and World War II in Southeast Missouri

An Autobiography by

Harvey D. Shell

Acclaim Press
MORLEY, MISSOURI

Acclaim Press
— Your Next Great Book —

P.O. Box 238
Morley, MO 63767
(573) 472-9800
www.acclaimpress.com

Designer: M. Frene Melton
Cover Design: M. Frene Melton

Library of Congress Cataloging-in-Publication Data

Shell, Harvey D. (Harvey Dean), 1933-
Whispers from the maple on the hill : life during the depression and World War II in southeast Missouri / by Harvey D. Shell.
p. cm.
Includes bibliographical references.
ISBN-10: 1-935001-13-2 (alk. paper)
ISBN-13: 978-1-935001-13-3 (alk. paper)
1. Shell, Harvey D. (Harvey Dean), 1933--Childhood and youth. 2. Dexter (Mo.)--History--20th century--Sources. 3. Dexter (Mo.)--Biography. 4. Dexter (Mo.)--Social life and customs--20th century--Sources. 5. Depressions--1929--Missouri--Dexter--Sources. 6. Nineteen thirties--Sources. 7. World War, 1939-1945--Missouri--Dexter. I. Title.

F474.D49S54 2008
977.8'95--dc22

2008047424

First Printing: 2009
Printed in the United States of America
10 9 8 7 6 5 4 3 2 1

Contents

Introduction

This book acknowledges my gratitude to those who surrounded me during my early years, and who are described in the episodes in this book.

This is a true story of events that I witnessed at a special place and time, and that have since evaporated into the mist of the past.

Those named in this story include both the living and the dead, and all remain in my fondest memories.

Special thanks are given to those who assisted me with the notes and pictures. Some of them were Florance Bright, Betty Allen, Charles Sitton, Faustina Barker, Lorena Eaker, Ronald Mouser, Alva Shell, Mary C. Shell, Carol Harris, William C. Shell, and Beverly Darter. Scott Swafford, Associate Professor, Missouri School of Journalism, advised me about the contents of the book.

I arrived in Old Dexter about 68 years after the end of the Civil War. My purpose in writing this history is to present my knowledge of the early part of the 20th Century, the Great Depression, the Roosevelt years, and World War II. I observed the arrival of the Works Progress

Administration, the Civilian Conservation Corps, World War II, and the medicine and technology being developed during that time.

This book is the story of my early life and my feelings about the events that took place during the years of 1933-1948. Prior to World War II, my family lived an almost communal life, similar to the way they had lived during pioneer times. Families assisted each other in all the general activities of life, especially in food gathering.

The global depression of 1929 began four years before I was born, and lasted until after the beginning of World War II. It was followed by the massive impact of the War itself that resulted in new ways of living, and the displacement of people from the area forever. Finally, the years just after the War were included to provide closure to the story. I have documented my remembrance of that era, and added my childhood interpretation.

The book also is also specific to the part of Missouri where I lived. Certainly, things were different in the larger cities.

I hope that this book projects the feelings of how it was to live on Crowley's Ridge during this tumultuous time in history, and the changes that have occurred.

Harvey D. Shell

The dream of life flows smoothly on,
like the breeze, which brushes past the dawn,
and finds itself among the leaves,
ignoring their chosen place of ease,
knowing not from whence it came,
to whom to give the praise or blame,
but moving onward in its flight,
waiting for another night.

Harvey Shell

Whispers from the Maple on the Hill

Life During the Depression and World War II in Southeast Missouri

Early Family History

The original location of the Shell family homestead is shown on the 1895 map[1] and drawing on page 14. The map also shows the locations of the birthplaces of my future wife, Joanne Bagby Shell, and myself.

My soul mate was born on August 18, 1936. The temperature was 108° F on that date. Her family had no electricity. Only cardboard hand fans were available for cooling. Global warming began on the day she was born.

Joanne Bagby

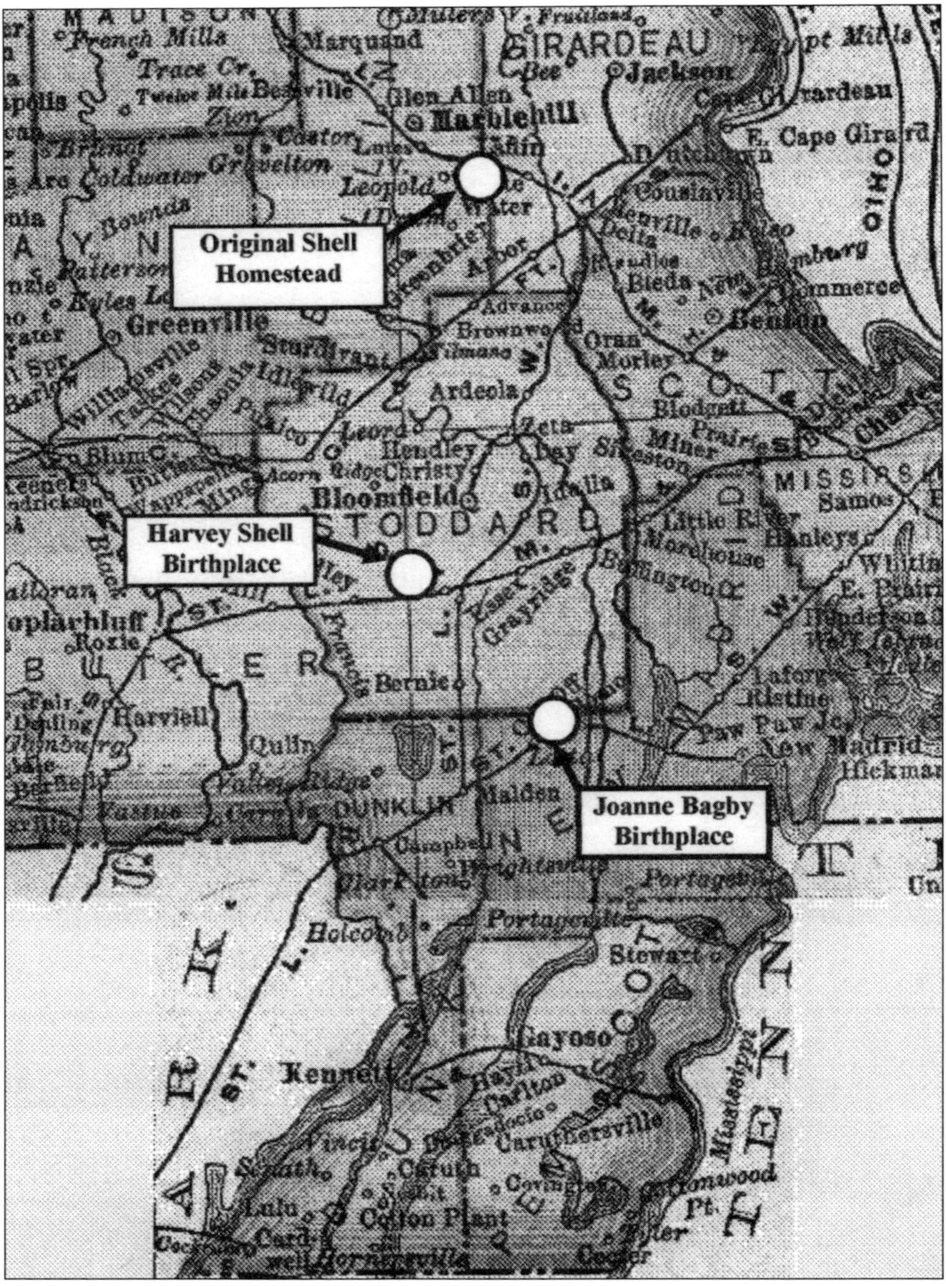

Map[1] of Southeast Missouri, 1895.

Original Shell Homestead

Uncle Wesley Shell was born in the original homestead house in 1854, and moved in the mid-1930s when the house became rickety. His grandfather, Casper Schell, had crossed the Mississippi in a wagon when he moved from North Carolina. He built the homestead with the help of others from Burfordsville. Uncle Wes told me stories about the early days and his memory of the militia riding down the road toward their house. My cousin Alva Shell recorded a long audio clip of Uncle Wes on his 100th birthday talking about the old days. I visited Uncle Wes in 1948 in the little house in the picture where he is sitting. I remember that Uncle Wes had Indian blankets and beautiful handmade furniture.

Uncle Wesley Shell

The original Shell homestead was built in 1804. It stood on a high slope, almost always visited by a breeze. Tall trees surrounded it, especially on the south and west sides. A bluff on the north side sloped down to the spring.

The house was built of logs,

S(c)hell Homestead

and wooden pegs were used instead of nails. Stones were used to make the fireplace, and to wall the spring. The first generation of children grew up and built their cabins along the side of the adjacent valley. The perpetual spring supplied pure, cool water to the families who lived there. They shared their efforts and crops with each other, and later rested together in the cemetery to the west. Their ancestors had lived about the same way through the centuries. In fact, my early years before WWII in Old Dexter were similar to theirs, and we had only a few additional mechanized improvements. The homestead structure lasted until 1938, enduring even the New Madrid earthquakes of 1810-1812 and the devastation of the Civil War.

The original builder was Casper Schell, Jr. The book, *The Shell Family*[2] by David L. Shell, describes in detail the building of the homestead and the construction of the spring enclosure. I do not know which Indian tribe was most involved in their lives. The Shawnee Indians were numerous in the area. The Cherokees were the dominant tribe in North Carolina where the family had previously lived.

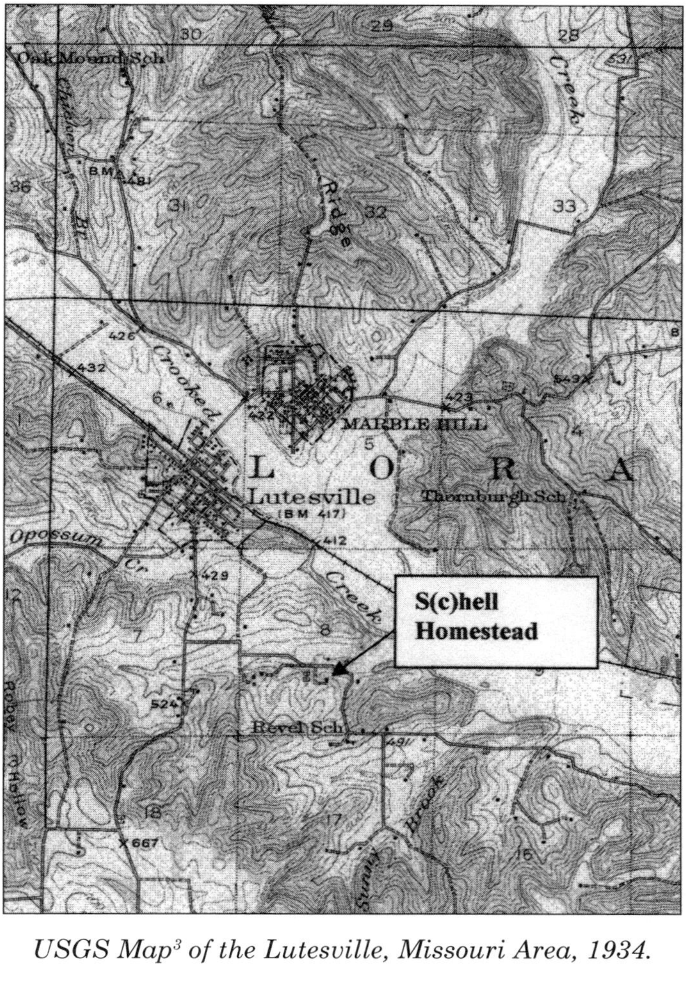

USGS Map[3] *of the Lutesville, Missouri Area, 1934.*

The homestead was still standing in 1934 when the following map was printed, and the home is shown as a dot at the end of the entrance road. The Shell Cemetery is shown just west of the homestead and to the left of the roadway.

According to my Uncle Wesley Shell, the Indians were there from the beginning. He said that the Indians had left the area before

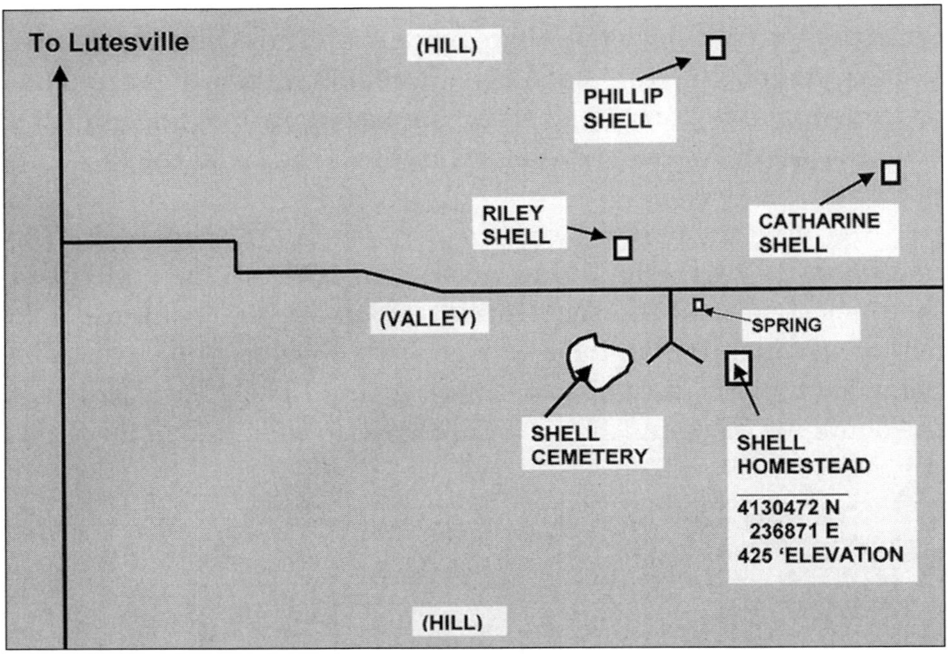

Homestead[4] Area Layout

he was born. He gave my dad a large iron skillet with three legs in which the original Shells had baked cornbread to share with the Indians. This was a frequent event according to Uncle Wesley, and the Indians became close friends with the S(c)hell family.

The book, *The Shell Family*[2] by David L. Shell, stated that the Indian neighbors helped care for Casper Shell's 17-year-old daughter Fanny, who was very ill. One night, according to family legend, a bright light appeared on the hill to the west. The Indians said that this was a sign that she was going to die, and that she should be buried where the light appeared. The next morning, she died, and was the first person to be buried in the Shell Cemetery.

When the Indians were leaving to move farther west, they confided that they knew where a silver mine was located on Crooked Creek. They said that they would show its location to the family. However, the Shells were afraid that the Indians might return someday and harm them in a robbery attempt. The offer was rejected. (This was my Father's version of the story. Lee Shell, a nephew of Wesley Shell, said that the mineral was lead instead of silver).

My Father donated the iron skillet to the Missouri State Museum in Jefferson City, Missouri. It was on display there until 1980. It has since been misplaced, and is among 65,000 artifacts stored there. It may show up in the future when the state lists all of its archived items on a computer database.

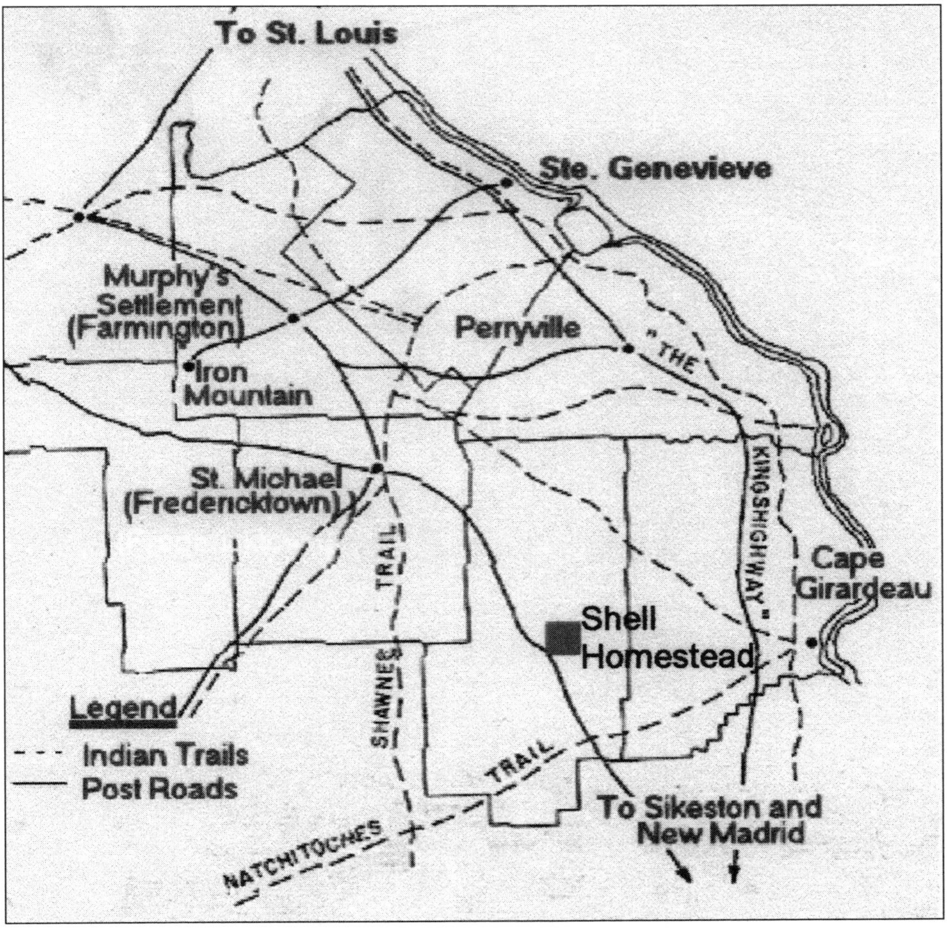

Indian[5] Trails

Pictures of my great-grandparents are shown on the following pages. They were not included in the Family Tree that follows, but I felt it appropriate to mention them. They were all born in the mid-1800s.

My Great Grandparents

Joseph P. and Sarah Harper Wright

Silas Harper and Beatrice Cook

Antney and Ruah Crites Shell

Caleb and Christina Inman Myers

FAMILY TREE[6, 7]

WILLIAM SHELL
(Grandfather)
LORENA (MYERS) SHELL
(Grandmother)

CHARLES CLEVELAND WRIGHT
(Grandfather)
RHODA (HARPER) WRIGHT
(Grandmother)

Harvey Shell
(Father)

Dottie Mae (Wright) Shell
(Mother)

Arthur & Willie Shell
Truman Shell
Alva Shell
Eleanora Shell
Gladys Elledge Shell

Early & Vernie Mouser
Leman Mouser
Perry Mouser
Virginia
Wilma

Neal & Minnie Mouser
John Mouser
Ronald Mouser
Neva Mouser

Bill & Sevia Shell
Beauton Shell
Faustina Shell
Eugene Shell
Imogene Shell

Elmer & Mary Shell
Clinton Shell
Vesta Shell

Johnson & Alta (Shell) Wiseman
Lola (Wiseman) Cook
Cecil Wiseman

Dora (Mouser) Lackey

Ina Shell

Paul & Mary (Shell) Sitton
Marian Lee Sitton
Charles Sitton
Ellen Sitton
Joyce Sitton

Worda & Rita (Render) Wright
Beverly
Bud
Jack

Charles & Virginia Wright
Beverly (Wright) Darter
Ronald Lee Wright
Jerry Wright

Lovie (Wright) & Noah Webb

Betty Jo (Wright) & Tom Allen
Tommy
Susan

Harvey Dean & Joanne (Bagby) Shell
Carol (Shell) Harris
Charles Alan

William Cleveland & Patricia (Duggins) Shell
Michael
Kimberly (Shell) Zellmer
Pamela (Shell) Klosterman

Crowley's Ridge

The place of my birth was on Crowley's Ridge in Dexter, Missouri. Our part of town was called Old Dexter, and my home was adjacent to the Old Bloomfield Road that extended along the crest. The road reached from Cape Girardeau, Missouri, to Helena, Arkansas, passing through Dexter, Missouri, and Bloomfield, Missouri.

Map[8] of Southeast Missouri (Shawnee Village), 1833.

It had once served as a game and Indian Trail, and passed by a Shawnee Indian village that was located Northwest of where Bloomfield now stands. The arrow on the map shows the location. It was near the center of Stoddard County and south of Castor River.

The Bloomfield Road carried troops to and from Arkansas into Missouri during the Civil War. A part of it followed the present highway 25 through Bloomfield; then it split off north of Dexter and followed a gravel road into Dexter.

The map below shows the approximate location of the Old Bloomfield Road, or Military Road. It was a major thoroughfare for

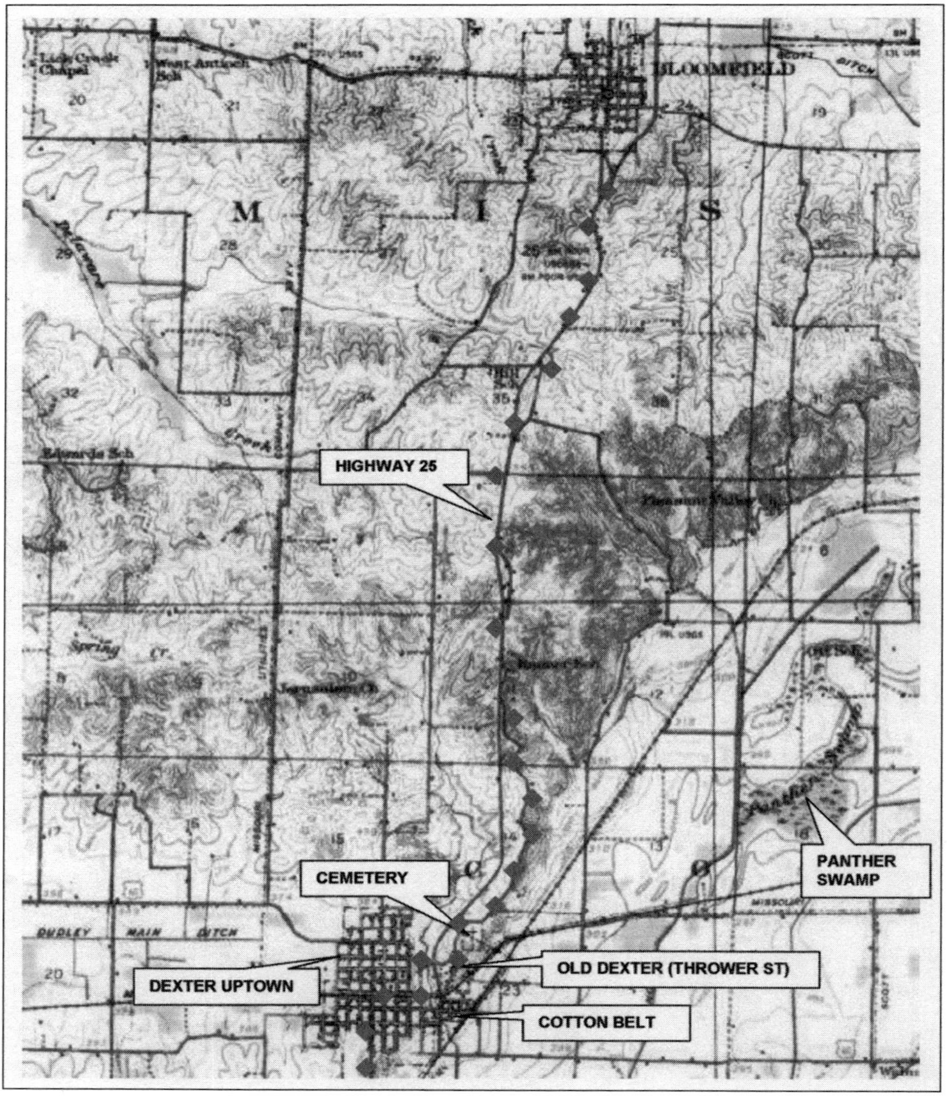

USGS Map[9] of Stoddard County, 1939.
The Old Bloomfield Road generally follows Highway 25.

all because it was higher than the swamps and lowlands around. During the New Madrid earthquake, the surrounding land east of Crowley's Ridge had sunk and was completely covered with water.

It was drained during the early 1900s. A diversion channel was constructed south of Cape Girardeau, Missouri, and connected to the Mississippi River. Flows from Castor and Whitewater Rivers were blocked, and their discharges were diverted eastward through the Channel into the Mississippi. The major flow from the North was thus stopped. A series of ditches were then constructed to drain the remaining water south. Much of the timber was cut, and new railroads constructed to carry the wood out. Little towns came into existence along the railroads. Water filled the ditches on each side of the narrow dirt roads, and beyond the ditches were wooded forests. A swamp to the east of Dexter was named the Panther Swamp. The Old Bloomfield Road in Dexter was about one hundred feet higher than the railroad and the swampland to the east. The railroad was about twenty feet higher than the swamp. Crowley's Ridge varied in width, and the width can be readily observed today from Highway 60 as one travels over it from east to west. The peak is where the Highway 60 intersects Highway 25 (in 2008). The land to the west drops off gradually as one crosses the Ridge, but remains higher than the land to the east, and continues on west to the Missouri Ozark Plateau.

A creek that runs south through Dexter divides the town. The newest part of Dexter was on the west side of the creek. Old Dexter was on the east side, resting on Crowley's Ridge, and the Cotton Belt was on the southeast corner resting in the flat, low land where two railroads entered the city.

A shirt factory, flour mill, railroad depot, churches, large grocery stores, the city hall, schools, armory lot, and primary shops were located in Dexter uptown. However, the grocery stores most convenient to old Dexter were in the Cotton Belt. A church, a handle factory, a railroad watering tank, a poultry processing plant, and later the airport were located there. The airport land and the armory Lot were vacant at that time. A baseball field was located on the airport land.

The railroad that ran west across Dexter was used as a main foot trail by many to get from old Dexter and the Cotton Belt to the shirt factory and uptown. Most of the people did not have cars; they walked to work. After the WPA program ended, my Uncle Bill Shell got a job with the railroad. He walked and carried his pick or shovel down and off Crowley's Ridge to his Cotton Belt work station.

The William Shell Family

Lorena Myers Mouser, who would be my grandmother, lost her husband and became a widow on February 5, 1905. She was left with three young children: Dora, Early, and Neal Mouser. Dora, the oldest, was only ten years of age, and the two boys were younger. All were too young to help much in the home or in the field. It was a very difficult time for her. People told her about an available widower, William Shell, who had recently lost his wife. He was trying to raise four children: Bill, Alta, Elmer, and Arthur Shell. While two of the boys were old enough to work in the fields, the other was not, and Alta, his daughter was only seven years of age.

They were both in need of someone to share their lives and help raise their families. However, Lorena could not find an occasion to meet William in the proper way she wanted. Like most women, she devised plans, imagined the proper dress and the most attractive way to make contact. The meeting could not be direct, but had to seem like it occurred by lucky chance.

One day, Grandma and Dora had climbed up into an apple tree and were picking apples. They were disheveled, sweating, and tired. Suddenly, amid a big swirl of dust, William Shell drove up in a buggy and started talking to Lorena. Her plans were completely abandoned as she climbed down and joined him. But the magic worked. They were married on December 6, 1906, and, to that union my father, Harvey Shell, Aunt Ina Shell, and Aunt Mary (Shell) Sitton were born. Grandma and Grandpa were very much

The William Shell Family
Bill, Alta, Elmer, Arthur, Dora, Early, Neal
Ina, William, Harvey, Lorena, Mary
Picture taken in about 1916.

in love, despite the awkwardness of their first meeting at the apple tree. The family that resulted is shown above.

The picture on the following page adds their spouses, and children.

The family moved about every two years and worked mostly in farming. Times were rough. They also ran a sawmill, and manufactured barrel staves and railroad ties. The family had a change in luck in 1915, and added stability to their lives. It provided cash flow for the family. It was a good venture for the family. Uncle Neal Mouser described it in his paper[10]:

> In September of 1915, my father took over the Star Mail Route (contract mail delivery) and a month later we moved to the Hahn, Missouri farm just south of the Hahn Post Office. My father, my brothers or I would deliver the mail by buggy six days a week, commencing at 7 AM. The Star

Back Row (from left): Bill Shell, Johnson Wiseman, Lola (Wiseman) Cook (baby), Alta (Shell) Wiseman, Elmer Shell, Arthur Shell, Thomas Lackey, Dora (Mouser) Lackey, Early Mouser, Vernie (Shell) Mouser, Neal Mouser; Middle Row: Mary (Conder) Shell, Clinton Shell, Willie (Francis) Shell, Harvey Shell; Front Row: Vesta (Shell) VanBibber (baby), Eleanora (Shell) Wilson, Truman Shell, Ina Shell, William Shell, Lorena (Myers) Shell, Mary (Shell) Sitton.

Route started at the Hahn Post Office, continued to the Sank Post Office, and then to Lutesville by around noon. After noon, the southbound train arrived, and the Lutesville Postmaster finished sorting the mail, we would start out for Hahn while delivering mail in small pouches along the way up to the bridge over Cane Creek. Then we would continue on to the Hahn Post Office where we would turn over the remaining mail. We would usually arrive back home before 6 PM. We lived on the Hahn farm until early spring of 1917 when my father bought a farm from Grant Galloway. While we lived on the Hahn farm, we attended the Eaker School during 1917, 1918 and 1919. My father sold the Star Mail Route in the fall of 1919.

Grandpa Shell was thinking about making a new investment, and was talked into moving to Arkansas by a good friend, Peter Eaker. Two of the children, Dora (Mouser) Lackey, and Early Mouser had moved to St. Louis. In February 1920, Grandpa Shell bought a farm about ten miles southwest of Paragould, Arkansas in the vicinity of Clarks Chapel School.

Crowley's Ridge was west and parallel to the St. Louis L & W Railroad, shown on the map on page 14. The area to the east was low swampland. The family loaded all their possessions onto a train and traveled to Delta, Missouri, where they boarded the L & W. The train followed Crowley's Ridge to Paragould, Arkansas. The men rode in the back of the train with their possessions, and the women and girls sat up front in the seats. My dad was very young, cold, and crying, and he was allowed to move up with girls.

The Paragould farm experience was kind of like moving into a depression, but twelve years before the actual big depression of 1929 occurred. Uncle Neal Mouser[10] described it this way:

> This small farm did not have very rich soil and did not produce a very good crop. Also, in 1920 the bottom fell out of the cotton market. Lint cotton dropped from 40 to 12 cents a pound, and my father, like most other farmers, decided to hold his cotton rather than sell. That made for hard times. There was no money to buy groceries that fall and winter or pay the grocery bills that had been charged throughout the summer.

People had very little money to buy anything extra, and they had to raise their own food. It got so bad that one couldn't even give away hay.

In the summer of 1921, a good crop was made, and things were better for the family. They rented another farm south of Paragould in 1922, and made another good crop. Things were improving, and Grandpa Shell was a happy person throughout the venture.

My father intensely disliked his stay in Arkansas. He felt that Grandpa had made a terrible mistake in moving to Arkansas.

It would be interesting to know what Grandpa and Grandma Shell were talking about above as they sat on the porch looking at each other.

Grandpa William and Grandma Lorena Shell at home in Arkansas, on the front porch of the Woods House where they lived.

The end view of the same house is shown in the following picture. Naomi McDaniel and Mary (Shell) Sitton are in the picture with hoes. Things were not too prosperous there. They posed with pipes in their mouths, although neither smoked.

End view of the Shell Arkansas Home Naomi McDaniel, Mary (Shell) Sitton

Despite the poverty, they did manage to purchase an old Model T Ford, and Grandpa made several trips back and forth into Bollinger County, Missouri, following the gravel road north along Crowley's Ridge.

Shown below is a 1915 Ford Model T Touring Car owned by Uncle Elmer Shell similar to the one purchased by Grandpa Shell.

At that time, Memorial Day was called Decoration Day. The churches would have big celebrations, and people would gather to visit and talk. They would place flowers and other decorations on the graves.

Grandpa would sit in the back seat of the car, relaxed, and my father would drive. He started driving when he was only thirteen years of age. There were no laws at that time for the age one could drive. The road was dusty, and the car was loud. It wasn't unusual to have ten or more flat tires during the trip. Grandpa wanted to get there fast, and he encouraged Dad to drive as fast as he could go along the bumpy gravel road. That is despite the probable tire blowouts that would occur. On one such trip, my Uncle Bill Shell traveled with them. Dad was going at top speed. My Uncle yelled "Stop this car; stop this car!!" He jumped out as soon as the car had stopped, ran down the hill, and collapsed. Grandpa and Dad followed him down to find out what was wrong. He said, "Harvey was driving so fast, I couldn't get my breath."

The Elmer Shell Family
Clinton, Mary, Vesta, Elmer

The Return to Missouri

In 1926, when my father was nineteen, the Shell family moved from Arkansas to Crowley's Ridge in Dexter, Missouri. Uncle Elmer Shell, a Baptist Minister, had bought a farm in Dexter. He had conducted revivals with his older brother, Arthur Shell.

It is likely that Uncle Elmer strongly influenced the family to move to Crowley's Ridge. Uncle Elmer always had some corn, milk cows, and ponies. He had a nice home and an automobile.

While he was still single, Uncle Bill Shell had spent one summer working for Elmer in Dexter. Again, most of the family settled together along the Bloomfield Road in "Old Dexter."

The close proximity of the family members allowed them to pool their resources and to support each other during the depression. This was similar to their way of living on the original homestead. In neither case did the families go hungry.

The following sketch[11] shows where the Shells located. They moved around from time to time, and different configurations on the sketch resulted from the moves.

The Old Bloomfield Road is on top of the Ridge, and Highway 25 slopes down off the Ridge as it goes south. I have shaded the Shell kinfolks' houses. The sketch is not to scale.

The railroad train whistles sounded both day and night and were something that we got used to. Smoke and soot were also present, and would soil the washed clothes that were hung on clotheslines to dry. Women would have to make sure that the wind was not blowing in their direction on washdays. Also, the

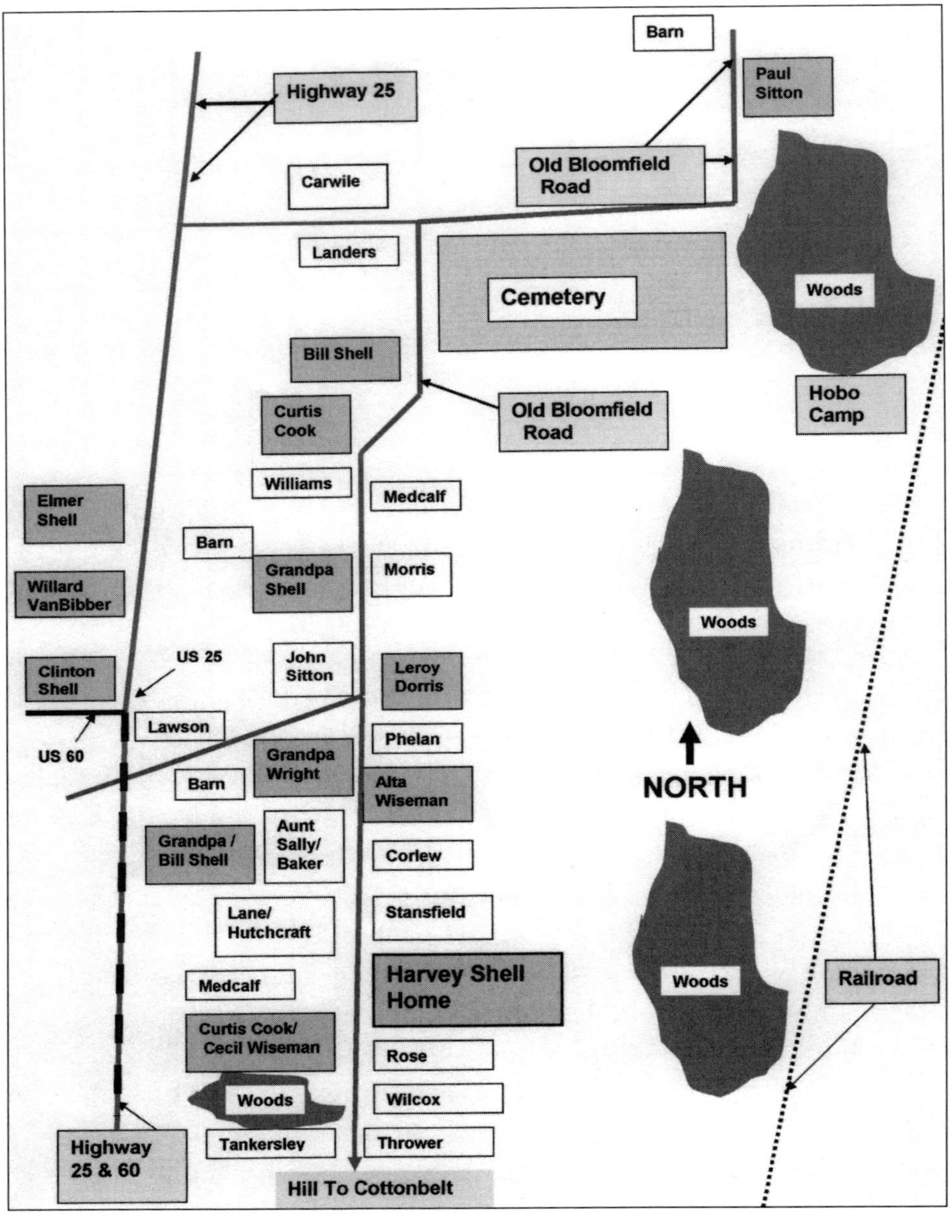

Layout Sketch[11] of Old Dexter (circa 1933-1947)

coal powered trains were louder than the diesel engines that came along later.

Uncle Bill Shell and Neal Mouser had married while in Arkansas. Uncle Neal had lived intermittently in St. Louis, Missouri.

Except for some part-time jobs, there was hardly any work available in Dexter. My father obtained a temporary job of cultivating some new land north of town. He would walk for three miles and begin plowing before daylight. He would work all day and walk home after dark. The pay was minimal.

Later, my father joined his sister, Dora Lackey, and his two brothers, Neal and Early Mouser in St. Louis to seek work. They had spent most of the Arkansas years intermittenly working in St. Louis. Jobs were available there, but times were rough. After the stock market crash, the jobs ended for all but Early Mouser.

The others gradually returned to Dexter for lack of work. Uncle Neal Mouser worked for McKinley Bridge Company, which almost went bankrupt, and his time was reduced to part-time. He could not afford to continue to work there. Dora Lackey had invested her money in the Stock Market, and lost most of it during the crash of 1929. My father, whose soda route job had ended, also left St. Louis and returned to Dexter for lack of work. He had planned on joining the Navy if he couldn't get a job. He did join the National Guard. A picture of the members at Camp Clark is shown below:

Missouri National Guard, 1932.
My Father is sitting in the second row, and 5th over from the left.

He took a course in cartooning, hoping that a job might develop from it. It was a natural thing for him to do. My father was very good at drawing and had an excellent handwriting. He was willing to do anything for wages. Unfortunately, nothing developed.

My Father's Cartoons

Some of his drawings are shown. The influence of the roaring 20s can be seen in the drawings. The drawings were all done with a straight pen, using India Ink.

And then a full-time position opened at the shirt factory where his two sisters, Ina and Mary were already working. Luckily, my father got a job there.

Sometime afterwards he met my mother. She was walking home from school and saw this handsome man with black wavy hair. She glanced at him, and then turned back. A second glance revealed that he was still looking at her. The intermittent glances evolved into a dating pattern. He married her when he was twenty-six years old and she was twenty-three. I entered the scene later.

Even though I was born during the rise of Adolph Hitler and the prelude to World War II, my early childhood was secure and happy. Our country was in the midst of the Great Depression, and many people were hungry, especially in the cities.

Yet, from my viewpoint, it was the best of times. Conversely, insecurity flooded my parents and other relatives. They were concerned with earning enough money to live, and providing bread for the table. The depression was worldwide, and the end of it could not be foreseen. The fear of war prevailed, and when World War II finally happened, millions of people died.

Nevertheless, my security was derived from my parents, my grandparents, and almost all my relatives who lived a short distance from me in Dexter, Missouri. I never did feel abandoned, or doubt that they loved me.

Awakening to Life

The sunlight was bright, except for short periods of rain showers that bathed the earth. Wild flowers abounded, and domestic perennials gathered to emit their sweet odors. Honeysuckles, lilacs and hollyhocks added their fragrance, and bees and butterflies scurried between them in a frantic passion not to miss one drop of nectar.

The birds and animals, not to be outdone, shouted their sounds and songs, both day and night. And the spring-like winds were warm with gentle expectation.

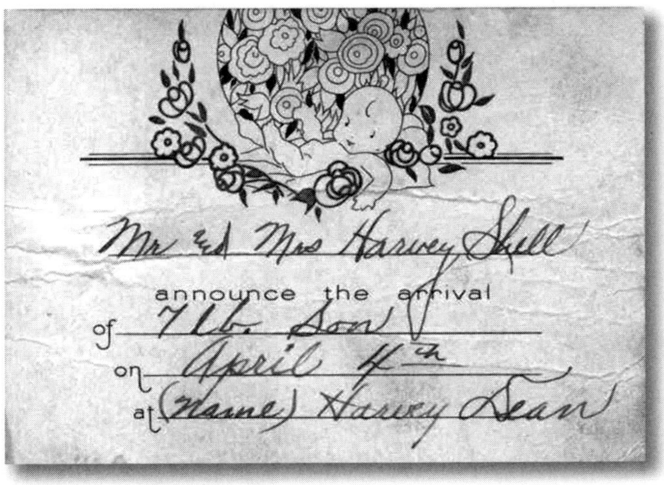

Mr and Mrs Harvey Shell
announce the arrival
of 7 lb. Son
on April 4th
at (Name) Harvey Dean

I entered this wonderful Eden on April 4, 1933. Dexter, Missouri was a very clean and prosperous town, and was growing. The new shirt factory, the two railroads, and the farming communities helped to offset the effects of the depression. And the schools provided a good place for me to live and learn. I would soon adapt to my wonderful surroundings, even though I knew nothing of them before I arrived. Love from the family would also soon be a priceless factor.

One of my earliest recollections was awakening to life, and saying to myself, "I am a person." I have often thought about this. Since I didn't have a language when I was born, it must not have occurred at the time of my birth. It may have been two or three years later when I fell off my dad's shoulders into a lake. I came up out of the water and saw light. Yet, it is possible that I later learned a language to fit my belief at the time of my birth.

My father was Harvey Shell (Sr.) and my mother was Dottie Mae (Wright) Shell. In the two pictures below are my Mother and her sister (Lovie). In the third picture, my Dad is with some of his nephews. In the fourth and fifth picture, Dad is with his sisters. He and Mother are then shown before they were married in the individual pictures. In the combined picture, they are in my Grandpa Shell's front yard after they were married. The road behind them and to the east is the Old Bloomfield Road.

Above and right: Dottie Mae Wright and sister, Lovie Wright.

Pictured from left: Harvey Shell, Cecil Wiseman, John Mouser,- Imogene Shell, and Eugene Shell.

Mary (Shell) Sitton, Harvey Shell and Ina Shell

Pictured from left: Joy Shell, Ina Shell, Harvey Shell, Mary Shell, and Dora Mouser.

Dottie Wright

Harvey Shell

Harvey and Dottie Shell

My father was masculine and decisive, and was my role model. He was very talented, and was respected by all who knew him. He had become a foreman of his section at the shirt factory. He played for a while on the Dexter Baseball team. He served on the City Council for a few years under Mayor Tommy Ross, and totally believed in Dexter as a city with a bright future. He supported many projects, including expanding the electrical and water

Dexter High School Teacher Training Class, 1929-1931.
Front row: Opal Jenkins – visitor, Blanch Loyd – teacher, Thurston (T.S.) Hill, Tom Book, Russell Coffey, unknown. Back rows: Verbie Hubbard, Wilma Littrell, Maureen Brennum, Dottie Wright, Wilma Allen, Ruth Norman, Gladys Kelly, Ruth Arnold, Grace Ross.

systems and fixing the roads, and he was an air raid warden. Some of the projects were coordinated with the WPA. His father-in-law, my Grandpa Wright, had also served on the Dexter City Council prior to my father's service.

My father spent quality time with me, and respected my opinions. He was inspirational, and ruled the household with dignity. My mother was gentle, and set high moral standards for the family.

Above is a picture of the Teacher Training Class that she attended in Dexter. Note that Thurston (T.S.) Hill is a member of this class. You could teach after graduating from Teacher Training.

Thurston Hill was a leader in education in the development of the Dexter schools. He eventually became Superintendent. He influenced the Missouri state school system when consolidation of public schools was active. The T.S. Hill Middle School is named after him.

My mother was a part-time schoolteacher. She was a substitute teacher for more than 50 years. She had a strong personality and would go to battle for her family for the slightest infraction. She supported the family with love and vigor. I still remember the opinions that she shared with me. She told me to always hold my stomach in, and I wouldn't get fat. She said that life is short, so live it with a smile, and don't develop any bad habits – they are hard to break. I listened, but tested her words throughout the years with some skepticism. Her greatest fear was of the Chinese, but I was never able to determine the reason. She also had phobias about foreign money and food.

Eyes of my parents and relatives were watching me from the time I left my house until I returned. It would have been hard for me to get into much trouble without a relative intervening.

My earliest days were spent in a house that we rented and shared with an old lady who took snuff (Aunt Sally). She was not related to the family, but everyone called her Aunt Sally. We were pretty cramped for space, but our family was small. Aunt Sally allowed us to live in the house rent free for taking care of her. She loved me, and held me as much as she could. I didn't mind the smell of snuff.

The house was just across the yard to the east of where my Grandpa and Grandma Shell lived with two of their grown daughters. Because we did not have an air conditioner, the windows were left open. We would have to swat mosquitoes every night, even though we had screens over the windows. One evening, Dad gave me a taste of juicy pork as a change to my milk diet. I had never tasted anything so good, and I loved it. Afraid that I would get choked, Dad removed it. I let out a scream so loud that my folks and all my neighbors could hear me, and Grandpa's family fell out in a run to my house to offer their help. They were surprised when they found that I was just having a tantrum (I got my licks in with the family early to get their attention).

Grandpa Shell was a baby boomer of the Civil War. His father, my Great Grandpa Antney Shell, was in the Missouri Militia. The Shells had no slaves, and like many of the people in the homestead area, they supported the Union Cause. The guerrillas in the area were a menace, and adult men had to either serve in the army or hide out for safety's sake. My Great Grandpa Caleb Myers could

Grandpa and Grandma Shell
William Shell and Lorena (Myers) (Mouser) Shell

not serve because of a club foot. He hid out in the woods during the daytime for the entire war. On one occasion, he went very deep into the woods and found a clearing to bed down. When he awoke the next morning, he found that he had slept in the middle of a road.

Grandpa Shell was born in 1866, a year after the war had ended. When he was about one year old, his mother, Mary Martindale, was thrown from a horse and killed.

Antney Shell had come home from the Civil War, married a very pretty woman, and sired a son. I am sure that he had dreams of a wonderful future life. He had a good life but not with Mary Martindale.

My Great-Grandmother and Great-Grandfather, Mary Martindale Shell and Antney Shell.

I don't know whether this was a wedding picture, or not, but it very well could have been.

Antney Shell died in 1930, three years before I was born, so I did not get to know him. I am told that he was a very meek man, somewhat withdrawing, but very nice.

The year 1933 was an exciting time for Grandpa and Grandma Shell. Grandma's birthday was on April 3, and I was born on April 4. Thirteen days later, my cousin Ronald Mouser was born. The picture shows Harvey and Ronald lying on a blanket.

Harvey Shell (left) and Ronald Mouser (right).

The view is to the east. The house and shed on the top left are part of the Aunt Sally home where I was born. The house on the right is across the Bloomfield Road. The garden and grape arbor are between.

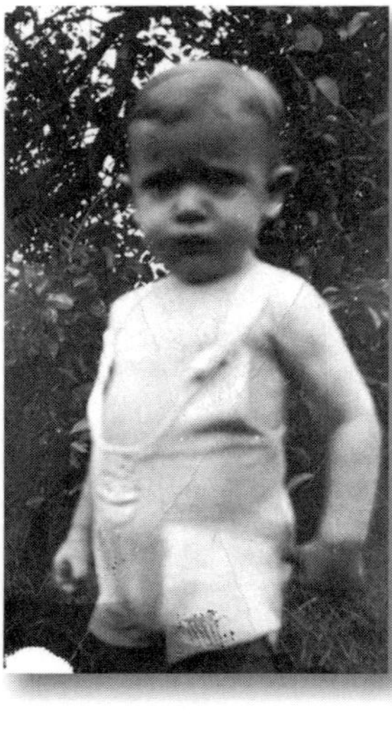

Harvey Shell

A few years later, my Aunt Alta lived in the Aunt Sally house. While living there, she married her second husband. Uncle Johnson, her first, had died. It was customary to have chivarees for newlyweds. And we had a big one for her.

She was a very vivacious woman, a big talker and the life of every party. All the family and friends gathered. Cigars were passed out, and there was plenty of food. Everyone laughed and talked. Supposedly, there would be tar and feathers, or riding the newlyweds on a rail at the end, but it never happened. One wonderful thing was that no one watched out for the kids. I was able to smoke a cigar with my older cousins in the shed.

My Grandpa and Grandma Wright lived north of the Aunt Sally home on a separate lot. We called them Dad and Mom. They had moved to Dexter from a farm in northern Stoddard County to make sure their children could attend high school, and they all did. Graduating from high school was quite unusual for people from rural Missouri at that time. He worked as a janitor at the school. Money was hard to come by during

Rhoda, Worda and Cleve Wright

The Wright Family
Worda, Dottie, Rhoda, Charles (front), Cleve, and Lovie

Railroad Culvert carrying water from the Dexter Creek - just west of previous picture view.

the Depression. Dad Wright always shared some food with a neighbor.

The top picture was taken in the Cotton Belt in about 1925 or 1926. The Wrights are facing south, and their Model T Ford is behind them. On the left side of the picture is Highway 60 with

Charles Cleveland Wright, Betty Jo (Wright) Allen, Rhoda (Harper) Wright

a sidewalk running north under a railroad trestle. The railroad runs east-west across Dexter. The large utility poles that followed the railroad probably carried electric power into Dexter from Cape Girardeau or beyond.

The family was younger in the first picture, and Betty Jo is missing from it. The picture at left shows Betty Jo.

At any rate, Dad Wright's youngest child Betty Jo looked upon me as a Godsend, especially for her. She carried me around, and shared me with her friends. She was a fan of Shirley Temple, and I became a substitute for her Shirley Temple doll. I learned the meaning of words from her including ghost, bomb, and mountain. I later practiced my counting in ones, fives and tens until I became proficient. The only prize that she refused me was her set of a glass cat and kittens. She was afraid that I would lose or break them, and told her mother to not let me play with them. It was the first thing that I would ask for when I visited them. Mom Wright could not refuse me. I finally broke one of them. I was always hungry when I visited, and would ask for a biscuit with mustard on it. Sometimes, a piece of bacon was available. If one was not available, a hug would do.

Betty Jo Wright and Harvey Dean Shell – year 1936.

The picture above was taken at the corner of the house where my Grandpa Shell first lived after moving back to Dexter. It is west of the Aunt Sally house where I was born. When he moved to his newer house, he sold the old home to my Uncle Early Mouser who lived in it for a short time. It was later occupied by my Uncle Bill Shell and his family. They called it the apple house because of the large orchard behind it. To the west of the house was a storm cellar. It was one of the first homes in Old Dexter that had electricity. The electric bill cost $1.00 per month.

Note that the view in the front right of the picture is from the top of Crowley's looking west toward the intersection of Highway 60 and 25. You can barely see Highway 60, as it comes east down the hill and crosses the Dexter Creek. The trees are along the Dexter Creek. The view as you descend the hill down Highway 60 shows advertisement signs along the east side of Highway 25. Dad later built a building that housed a restaurant on the east side, and rented it out for several years. There were no buildings on the lot on the west side.

At that time of the picture, Highway 60 came into Dexter from Poplar Bluff to the west, proceeded through North Dexter, crossed a bridge over the Dexter Creek, turned south to the Cotton Belt.

It then turned east toward Sikeston. Highway 25 came into Dexter from Bloomfield to the north, turned west at the Dexter Creek bridge, proceeded up the hill to Walnut Street, turned south on Walnut Street, and though the town, off the hill and onward to Bernie. It later by-passed uptown Dexter, and followed Highway 60 where it connected with the Bernie highway.

The shirt factory opened a new plant in Kennett, Missouri, and my father was given the opportunity to move into an advanced position. He discussed this with the family. It was a big decision, since the family stability was based in Dexter. We were with our grandparents and other relatives about every day.

Lola Cook

The Maple Tree waved in disbelief that we would even discuss leaving old Dexter.

Lola (Wiseman) Cook and her husband, Curtis Cook, were much impressed. They wanted to go with us, and the two families moved south. I was 2-1/2 years old. We were all very short on cash. Curtis and Lola had only $5 to make the move. On the way down, we stopped at a roadside stand to look at chalk cats and other items. The vendor was a good salesman, and sold Lola a chalk cat for $3.50. Well, it was tough going for a while, and the only meat on the table was bologna. Somehow, we managed to survive. The jobs were not satisfactory, and everyone was very homesick. One day my Mother found me in the back yard standing by the water pump. I had gone to sleep standing up. That was the last straw. Everyone moved back to Dexter, and my father got his job back at the factory. After trying several jobs, Curtis Cook entered the Nazarene ministry, and remained true to it for the rest of his life.

A Home Under the Maple on the Hill

My father purchased an old house on Crowley's Ridge that we shared with the renters, Mammy Rose, Junior, Ida and Eva. It was down the street from the house where I was born. There were many snakes, with one passing through the yard every week or so. My mother was horribly scared of snakes. One even rolled off the back porch roof in front of her. However, each scare was short lived. Mammy Rose kept a sharp garden hoe by the back porch, and had a terrific aim.

There was an outside water faucet with city water at the back corner. There were two washtubs for the Monday morning clothes washing. One day, Mom found me holding a kitten under the water to see if it could swim like a catfish. She pulled it out just in time.

The old abandoned building in the back served for a short time as a hiding place for buried bootleg whiskey owned by some of my relatives. Dad let them use it for a while, but after the liquor had all been dug up, he closed the operation, and let it be shut down.

Prohibition had ended the year that I was born.

Dad built a new house adjacent to the old, and we moved into it before I was four years old. All of the family possessions were carried by hand from the old home to the new.

It was a grand structure in comparison to the old house. Dad was a good carpenter. Power tools were not available, so Dad used manual hand tools, and he was able to buy cement, lumber and nails. He used a brace-and-bit for drilling holes, a handsaw for cutting wood, a level for leveling the structures, a square for aligning the boards, a rule for measuring, and a plane for smoothing the boards.

In addition to the new house, Dad built a one-room gasoline filling station at the intersection of Highway 60 and Stoddard Street. He hired my Uncle to run it during the day, and he helped at night. One night, they thought that a car transporting the gangster Pretty Boy Floyd had purchased gas from them. There was no Highway Patrol at that time, and they could never find out. The filling station venture was not very profitable. Later, the station was shut down, and the building was expanded on each end and rented as a single building.

Bootheel gasoline station showing the additions on each end.

The vertical gasoline tanks were abandoned. Some boys who were burning grass on the ditch bank let the fire get too close to the tanks. People were napping in Dexter after church, and after having had a full Sunday dinner. Suddenly, a loud explosion shook the buildings all over town. It blew a manhole cover off of one of the tanks that traveled for over a quarter of a mile into a man's front yard. No one was hurt.

Our new house did not have indoor plumbing. It was quite easy to carry water each day over from the outdoor faucet at the old house to the new. My ancestors had to carry water from a spring.

Having city water was a big improvement over the wells that some of the neighborhood had. We had a water bucket with a dipper for drinking, and a wash pan for our hands. The toilet was outside the house, as was the case for all the homes in the neighborhood. The overall situation was not too different from that of the homestead days. We used newspapers and sales catalogues for toilet tissue. I don't know what they used in the homestead days.

The house was rectangular in layout. We entered it from the door on the southeast corner of the front porch. A swing was on the north end of the porch. The front two rooms of the house were only partially separated. A single electric light hung from the ceiling on a long cord in the center of each room. A pot-bellied stove was near the center, and the water bucket and wash pan were on a small table in the rear corner. We also had a table and chairs, a couch, and a radio.

The radio was a large upright console with a button in front to turn it on and adjust the volume, and a second button for tuning it. The main radio station was KWOC in Poplar Bluff, and we set the tuner there most of the time. It was about the only station that we could get.

All of the men in the neighborhood would visit us and gather around the radio when Joe Louis fights occurred. Joe Louis was our favorite boxer and hero. Loud cheers would go up when Joe struck a blow.

Two small side rooms of our home contained a kerosene cookstove and an icebox. Our two bedrooms with single electric lights were in the rear. They opened onto a concrete slab and small porch. Three pear trees, a peach tree, and a plum tree were planted in the back yard. I spent a lot of time up in the trees. Other assorted trees, shrubs, and flowers were scattered around.

The toilet was near the back corner of the lot, and a fenced hog-pen was farther back. Dad later built a combination garage and meat storage building on the south east side. A coal pile and a stack of lumber were next to the backside of the building.

The garage also served as our bathhouse during the summer. We would draw the water and take baths in a galvanized tub. During the summer, the tub was placed outside, and the water would heat up in the sun. We would then pull the tub into the garage, close the doors and bathe. In the winter we would bathe inside the house. We would heat some water and add it to the tub. Normally, we would bathe in the front room near the pot-bellied stove.

We would wash our feet daily in a wash pan and use soapy washcloths to clean the dirt from our face and arms.

Our new house had two large maple trees in the front yard, one larger than the other. During that time, the Carter family was singing on the radio "Beneath the Maple on the Hill." It was my mother's favorite song, and she often sang and hummed it.

I cannot think about the home place without including the taller of the two maples. I climbed it, sat under it, played with my toys, and sometimes napped under it. If a pallet were made and I had a large cold soda, I could pass a summer afternoon under it in peace. My choice was a large Pepsi Cola. The radio played "Pepsi Cola hits the spot / twelve full ounces, that's a lot / twice as much for a nickel too / Pepsi Cola is the drink for you."

Generally, on those hot days, my neighbors were resting next door under their trees. The adults and children shared the pallets.

My family sitting in a chair under the Maple Tree.

The Maple on the Hill[12]

1. Near a quiet country village stood a maple on the hill,
there I sat with my Geneva long ago.
When the stars were shining brightly we could hear the whippoorwill,
and we vowed to love each other evermore.

2. Don't forget me, little darling, when they've laid me down to rest,
just one little wish, darling, that I pray.
As I linger there in sadness thinking, darling, of the past,
let your teardrops kiss the flowers on my grave.

3. We would sing love songs together when the birds had gone to rest,
we would listen to the murmur of the hill.
Will you love me, little darling, as you did that starry night,
as we sat beneath the maple on the hill.

4. I will soon be with the angels on that bright and peaceful shore,
even now I hear them coming o'er the hill.
So goodbye, my little darling, it is time for us to part,
I must leave you and the maple on the hill.

The Maple Was Smiling

To understand me, one must look in all directions from the large maple tree. It was the center of my territory. It contains the early memories and dreams that I experienced. The tree still whispers to me if I listen closely.

From a branch of the tree, look north up the gravel road, and see me playing in my Grandpa Shell's yard. He had since moved to a better home about one-quarter of a mile farther north.

The beautiful house below is the one that he purchased. It was tough during depression times to make a cash purchase for anything.

Grandpa's house.

However, he bought the home for a reduced price from Clarence Powell, a local Attorney at Law. The house had been owned by a family who lost it for failing to pay the real estate taxes.

My grandpa sat in a chair with a walking cane across his legs, and enjoyed the company of his grandson. He was excited and awaited the news of a new arrival to the family. It was March 24, 1937.

Suddenly my father appeared, and my grandmother and aunts also joined him in the yard. He talked briefly with them, smiling, and waved me to follow him home. He said that he had a big surprise for me, and asked me to guess what it was. I guessed that it was candy, a pet, and toys, but father kept saying, "It is better than that." When I got home, I found my mother in bed with a little red-faced baby. In that day, babies were born at home, and not always with a doctor present. In my case, Dr. LaRue was in attendance, and in the case of my baby brother, Dr. Davis attended. I was lifted up onto bed, and Dad said, "Your big surprise is a little brother." That was my brother Bill. I wanted him to get up and start playing with me immediately, but of course that couldn't happen. I decided to give him a toy. That was a big decision – I didn't have many toys. Finally, I found a worn-out, molded paper Easter rabbit that had been given to me by my Aunt Lovie, and I lovingly gave it to him. That was not a problem since the candy from its basket had already been eaten, and I was tired of the rabbit. Yet, it was an unselfish act of sharing with him, and I have continued giving freely to my brother Bill throughout the years.

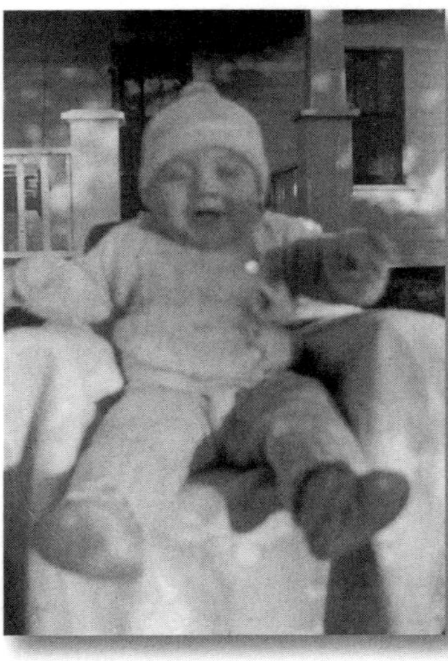

Bill Shell

Harvey and brother Bill

That event did not spoil me, and I was not a crying brat. My parents, grandparents, aunts, uncles, and cousins always gave me everything I wanted, and I had no goals blocked. No need to cry. What a great way to raise a kid.

And Bill waxed strong. He was first on mother's milk, and when he grew older, my mother would chew the solid food, and place it in his mouth. No commercial baby food was available at that time. Later, before he could count, he would lay out the number of bacon rinds by his plate to match the number with Dad's. He would make sure that the number was the same or greater.

Mother took Bill and me to the funeral of my Great Grandmother Wright. I had not been to a funeral before, so I watched with awe. I could remember my Great Grandma well. She had lived in a neat little house with a front porch. In her garden some unusual plants grew, mixed with the garden vegetables. I was told that it was tobacco. She sometimes chewed a plug of it, as she rocked on the front porch.

Sarah Wright (my great grandmother)

The funeral service began, and Bill got down under the church pew and started crying. Mother couldn't get him out. She discretely tried every way to remove him, and would pause, and try again. And he started crying louder, and kicking the wooden braces under the pew. His behavior went on until the end of the service. I had never seen my Mother so frustrated.

Harvey and Bill Shell

In the picture above, the Old Bloomfield road (Thrower Street) is directly behind us.

Harvey and Bill Shell

There is a line of trees along the road. Our car is behind us on the right, and the driveway is connected to the Old Bloomfield Road. The Maple on the Hill can be seen over the top of the House. The driveway slopes downhill to the west. The yard was well kept and pristine behind the boys along the street.

On one occasion, my Dad had driven my Grandpa Shell to town, and on the way home had stopped at our house. He left the Ford Coupe in the driveway. Grandpa Shell remained in the car, while Dad went into the house. My Brother Bill got into the car, and sat down in the driver's seat. Suddenly, Bill accidentally released the emergency brake. Grandpa yelled as the car rolled backward, down the driveway, across the road, and into a neighbor's yard. No one was hurt, but there were two big sets of eyes very wide open when Dad finally caught up with them.

My Mother stayed at home with us before World War II, and did not have a job. That was the case of most of the married women of that time. She did the cleaning, canning, washing, ironing and cooking. It was a full day's work. A clothesline was used for drying the clothes.

She taught us all the nursery rhymes, and read to us continually. We would sit with her and listen to her read our favorite poem, "Enoch Arden," by Alfred Lord Tennyson. We would cry along with her every time we heard it.

She sometimes sang, "Froggy went a courting, and he did ride, uh-huh, Froggy went a courting and he did ride, uh-huh, Froggy went a courting, and he did ride, a Sword and a pistol by his side, uh-huh---." It went for twenty or more verses, and Bill and I loved it.

Depression Food

Springtime burst forth every year with the energy of resurrection. Activities were expedited as all were inspired by the new life. My birthday occurred every April with presents. Wonderful!

My uncle, Noah Webb, was a blacksmith, and his shop was filled with people ready to begin spring planting. A checkerboard was placed on a nail keg with players and observers standing around. My uncle's forge was going, and the clanging of his hammer and the follow-up sounds of the quenching of the hot steel in water filled the air. I enjoyed the special smell of the shop operation that was bittersweet, yet a pleasant odor. Horses hitched to wagons outside the shop stomped their feet restlessly, snorted, and rattled the harness. My uncle sharpened plow points and occasionally went outside to nail on horseshoes. The men talked about farming, told stories about people, family, preachers, jobs, horses, and other events, and laughed. The boxer Joe Louis was often the subject of interest. The stories were generally clean enough for young boys like me to listen to. The preliminary work was done, and the show was ready to begin.

In a few days, wagons banged, and clattered down the gravel road in front of my house. And suddenly one of them turned into the yard. It stopped banging as it turned into the dirt driveway. Dad ran out to meet it, and I followed closely. The wagon was narrow with a single horse pulling it. It had a plow and a harrow in it. We called a harrow, a "harr," and that one was homemade. It was V-shaped, made of railroad ties with large spikes sticking through them to break up the clods. I watched intently as the garden was plowed, harred, and made ready for planting. The wagon was then loaded with the equipment and taken away.

Dad proceeded later with a garden plow, and soon furrows were scattered across the area. Lettuce, onions, radishes, carrots, cucumbers, and peppers were planted. Peas and green beans were planted, and poles to support them were inserted. I just couldn't fathom the efforts, and what new things would transpire. All of a sudden, the plants were loaded with vegetables, and the wonder of nature abounded. Mother cooked the peas with a little milk, salt and flavoring, and served lettuce, wilted with pork grease and onions, and made biscuits and mashed potatoes. It was amazing to me that we could raise our own food in a garden.

Most of my family in town was still into farming of one kind or another as a way of life. About everyone had chickens; some had hogs and milk cows. My Uncle Elmer had corn, and my Uncle Paul Sitton had strawberries and sweet potatoes.

Picking strawberries at Paul Sitton's Farm on Crowley's Ridge. Back row from left: John Sitton, Mary (Major) Shell, Maggie Davis, Lorena Shell, George Morris and Ralph Morris. Front row: Paul Sitton, Johnson Wiseman, Alta Wiseman, Kathleen Allen, Lola Wiseman, Vesta Shell, and Mary Sitton.

Notice that the men were wearing hats, and the women were wearing bonnets. The dress style was denim overalls for the men and long white dresses for women. It applied when working outside, (and sometimes inside, and sometimes even for church.)

A truck was a must for farm work. It was used for the strawberry harvest, hog killing, and all the other activities on the farm.

Below are some pictures of the truck.

Above: Paul Sitton's Truck. George Morris and Paul Sitton.

Left: Vesta Shell and Lola Wiseman.

Grandpa and Grandma Shell had a large garden and a milk cow. Grandpa raised bees, and had several hives. Some of the family did not have electricity, and used wood for fuel and heating. We were in the minority with electric lights, and we purchased coal for fuel from the nearby railroads. The coal smoke from the stoves added to that of the trains, and was very dense and strong.

The family would work together to supply food for all, much like our ancestors did before us. According to my Uncle Wesley Shell who was born in the Homestead house in 1854, the fertility of the soil made it possible for the pioneering families to survive. They did not have plows, but used grubbing hoes for planting. He said that one could stir up the soil, and spread a few beds of seeds. From these, lush crops of corn, beans, pumpkins, and potatoes would grow. There were so many pumpkins that they would feed the extras to the cattle. The chickens and hogs lived in the woods. The families shared the food and water and survived.

Bill Shell in Grandpa Shell's front yard.

The picture above shows that my brother Bill was involved in canning beets. His mouth and hands were completely covered with red stains. The Old Bloomfield Road is behind him, and the Morris home is directly across the road.

During the Depression, my grandfather had enough potatoes and honey for all the families. The potatoes were stored in his cool half-cellar, and divided among the families. Grandpa would sometimes reapportion the number of potatoes in each bin, depending on the need.

My Grandma Shell and other family members made sauerkraut, head-cheese, lard, and soap. They dried apples, peaches, canned beets, beans, other vegetables, and pork sausage. I really liked the sausage that was canned in lard. WOW!!, it was good. Don't worry about the cholesterol. All the families had individual gardens for their own needs. The canning season would follow the strawberry harvest in late May, and the vegetable and fruit tree harvest in late summer. Those activities were repeated every year.

Hogs were killed and butchered as a community project, generally on Thanksgiving Day. All of the original activities took place in Grandpa Shell's yard. Later, other people joined in and the work was transferred to the Morris yard across the street.

"Hog Killing" in Morris Yard

Pictured from left: Early Mouser, Piggy, Arlie Lawson, John Sitton, Bill Shell, Paul Sitton, and Frank Morris. George Morris (kneeling).

The operation continued to grow, and it was moved to Uncle Paul Sitton's farm north of the Cemetery. The pork was smoked and salted to preserve it for the year. Grandpa made headcheese as a specialty. We kids were also given cracklin's and pigtails to eat. It was a treat for us, as was the entire hog killing event. The kids could do about anything they wanted while the adults worked, since they were too busy to supervise. My brother fell off a haystack and broke his arm one year.

The Old Bloomfield Road was in front of Grandpa Shell's new home, and the Morris home was across the street. Mr. Frank Morris would sit on the front porch every day during the summer and listen to the St. Louis Cardinals baseball game on the radio. He would get excited and cheer them on at times. He would even jump up and down.

Mrs. Nova Morris tended to her chores, one of which was feeding chickens.

The picture below was taken behind the Morris House. Many of the people in Old Dexter raised chickens during the Depression.

Feeding chickens.

When Grandpa Shell first moved into his newer house, it was rumored that gold was buried somewhere in the yard. My father purchased an auger, and holes were bored throughout the yard without success. Someone heard that there was a mystic near Dudley, Missouri that might be able to help us. Some of the Shell family visited his dark swamp home near Dudley, and he could immediately tell them detailed stories about their lives even though he had never met any of them before. He was prepaid for his services. He said that he could see gold in the yard at the southeast corner of the house. Well, they rushed home and started digging immediately. It was said that gold would sometimes move underground, if it was about to be disturbed. They finally found a cache of bottles and tin cans where they dug, but no gold. Nothing was ever found, and the gold fever finally died out.

During the family visits, the men would often sit on the front porch and smoke. That is all except for Grandpa Shell. He did not smoke.

Dad and Mom Wright moved back to the farm in 1939. The entire family is shown in the picture just before they moved. You will note that by this time, there is a fire water hydrant. The old Bloomfield road turns down the hill on the creek road on the left side of the picture. You can't see the road. It is behind the raised corner.

The Wright Family in 1939 in Dexter

Back row from left: Bill Shell, Dottie Shell, Worda Wright, Dad Wright, Mom Wright, Charlie Wright, Noah Webb. Front row: Betty Jo Wright, Harvey Shell, Harvey Dean Shell, Lovie Webb.

Ms. Phelan lived across the road behind the water hydrant. The Morris family lived on the left side of the picture in the white house.

The farm land adjoined Castor River. According to records that I have reviewed, the Harper family name had an Irish origin. According to Robert Houck's history[13], Robert Harper had settled on Castor River near Zalma, Missouri, and Black Mingo Swamp prior to 1803.

The old house in the picture below (the Hardy Place) was the one where Mom (Harper) Wright was born. She is sitting on the front porch with Betty Wright, and holding Bill Shell. The picture was taken between 1938 and 1939.

Mom Wright's birth place.

When she was only five or six years old, Mom Wright lost her mother. The only memory that she had of her mother was sitting on her lap. She said it gave her a warm feeling. Her mother, Beatrice Cook Harper, was born in 1861 and died at the age of thirty-four in 1895. Several children and Mom's father, Silas Harper, were left behind. Silas kept all of the children together and they lived on this farm. Two of the older boys helped their father in the fields and another, Edgar Harper, stayed inside and kept house. He cooked and took care of the younger children.

Grandma Rhoda Wright's Mother, Beatrice Cook Harper

On one occasion, a dog with rabies got under the floor of the old house and bumped up the loose boards in the floor. It was very scary for Mom Wright and her sisters until the men returned from the field and killed it.

Silas Harper was remarried about a year later to Grandma Becky Jenkins, and they had three children.

Grandma Becky felt that Mom (Harper) Wright was spoiled. One example was that Mom Wright did not like the fat on her meat. She was told that she could have no more meat unless she ate all the fat on the first piece. She refused. Grandpa Silas Harper solved the problem. He would eat the remaining fat on her first piece, and give her another. Grandma Becky was not happy about that, and continued to believe that she was spoiled.

I have inserted a 1939 map[9] (see page 74), and marked the area (1st Farm) to where they moved. The old house shown in the picture on page 72 was replaced before school started in 1939. It was north of Bloomfield, and west of Aquilla. One note of interest is that Highway 25 did not extend north of Aquilla at that time. To reach Advance, Missouri, one would drive north of Aquilla and follow the unpaved roads up through Gravel Hill.

The farm was close to Castor River. Castor River was a favorite of my father's. It only had a slight flow since the upper part of it had been cut off. He would take me along on his frequent visits, and we would fish and sightsee.

He bought a canvas canoe that had completely rounded out of its original elliptical shape, and appeared to be unstable. The canvas was made waterproof with varnish. It was first tested in a drainage ditch east of Dexter. A neighbor said that he knew a lot about canoes, and bragged that he could handle it. His actual background was one of drinking liquor and prize fighting. A whole group of men traveled to the ditch to observe the test, and placed their bets. It was on a cold day, so they built a fire on the ditch side.

Our neighbor got into the canoe, and the men cheered him as he was shoved out into the ditch. After three or four strokes of the paddle, the canoe turned over in the cold water. He plunged in head over heels. They got him ashore, placed him by the fire, and covered him up. With the warmth and pre-test antifreeze in his body, he survived.

My father kept the canoe and learned to maneuver it quite well. I don't know of a time that he turned over. I rode with him much of the time. A few life preservers were being used at the time in small boats. Those that existed had cork as a floatation media. We could not afford to use life preservers in our canoe.

Castor River Farms, 1939 USGS Map[9]

The family built a cabin next to Castor River, and we enjoyed it. My uncles spent quite a lot of time there. I remember camping up there, but we had no water well. We dipped water from Castor River and boiled it with the coffee in the pot.

Sometimes we swam. Mosquitoes and hot weather demanded it. On one occasion, the men disappeared down the river and went skinny dipping. The women went swimming near the cabin. They pinned their skirts at the bottom with safety pins and swam with their clothes on.

The Model 35 Ford coupe in the picture belonged to my Aunt Lovie and Uncle Noah Webb. We had one too, but it was not as sophisticated. Uncle Noah's had a rumble seat that folded into the trunk. One could raise it up and out, and could ride in it. Since the standard coupes had only a front seat, a third seat came in handy at times.

The following pictures show some of the family near the cabin.

Harvey, and my brother Bill Shell on our dad's shoulder.

Harvey, Bill, Dottie Shell and Lovie (Wright) Webb.

Bill Shell

Noah Webb, Bill Shell

One big event that I remember at the old farm occurred in the summer of 1941. The family was sitting in front of the house, and Charlie Wright's car came pulling up. That was not unexpected since he lived there. The car parked at a distance next to the west fence. He and a girl, Virginia Clark, whom he had been dating, climbed out. They would not talk, and only giggled. They would not answer our questions. They departed toward the backside of the house, and everyone followed. When we finally caught up with them, questions erupted. "Did you get married? I'll bet you got married. What's going on?" Finally, they confessed that they had been married in Piggott, Arkansas that afternoon. Everyone congratulated them and celebrated. At that time, Arkansas had no marriage rules, and many Missouri couples went to Piggott to get married. It was the closest Arkansas City, and there was no waiting time.

This union was indeed a miracle. Virginia had been on the racing team in school, and was the fastest runner in Dexter. At eighteen years of age, she was too fast for any man to catch, even when she was running at half speed. Along came Charlie who was twenty-two years of age, and he was successful. Maybe she just slowed down. Or maybe he was fast too. He had long legs.

Virginia (Clark) Wright and Charles Wright

Charles Wright

Dad and Mom Wright moved to another farm (the Lewis Place) south of Castor River to a location about two miles west of Aquilla (2nd Farm). The location is also shown on the map on page 74. The two-story house faced an abandoned road to the north. An old log barn was also located on the property. Dad Wright hired a moving crew to come in and to place the house on rollers. They turned the house around, and rolled it to the south so it would face a new farm-to-market road being built. Dad Wright owned the property on both sides of the new road. He and one helper built a new house there to replace the old one at the end of the war.

One event occurred at this farm that I remember vividly. I had started playing with matches, and could find no other pleasure so great. I was in the smoke house, and found a box of matches. No one was around, so why not? After striking a few, I dropped one on the floor, and it started burning profusely on the grease soaked boards. I ran into the house, and shouted that the smoke house was on fire. Everyone emptied the house quickly, and rushed outside to put it out. They discussed how the fire might have started. My Uncle Charlie Wright said that a mouse may have ignited the box. "They sometimes do you know," He said. After listening for a while, and building up pressure inside, I yelled loudly, "I did it!" After a moment's hesitation, everyone laughed, and my Uncle Charlie laughed the loudest of all.

I have many memories of that farm. They raised corn and hay, planted a big garden, and had fruit trees. They had chickens, milk cows, and hogs. At that time, a small farm of 80 to 120 acres would support a family well. They got up early each morning before daylight, milked the cows, gathered the eggs, and made a large breakfast. They would sometimes squirt the milk at my mouth, or toward the cat. Mom would cook a whole platter of eggs, some hard, some over easy, and we could scoop out as many as we wanted. We also had homemade biscuits with butter, ham or bacon, gravy, jelly, and hot black coffee.

The late Depression food was generally not too bad. We did not suffer the Depression nearly as badly as those living in the cities. However, there were times when we did have to subsist on fried bologna, and the evening meals consisted of only cornbread and milk. We later learned that some of our neighbors had experienced hunger. We fed others, including hobos who came by, begging for food. They would always come to the back door, and my mother never refused them. We had a hobo camp down the hill from the southeast corner of the Dexter Cemetery. It was adjacent to the railroad that ran nearby. At this time railroads were very prevelant. Anybody could hop a train and travel to most small towns in the country. We would spy on the hobos. They cooked some of their food in large cans, and savory smoke wafted from the camp. They slept, smoked, and sometimes argued. There were generally five or six hobos present. They never let on that they observed us, and maybe they didn't.

For cash flow on the farm, Grandma and Grandpa Wright separated the cream from the milk with a mechanical separator that they used every morning. They sold the cream along with the eggs in Bloomfield on Saturdays. From this money, they bought flour and other necessities. The flour bags had decorations, and could be used to make clothing. It was not unusual to see women wearing flour sack dresses.

The wood for heating and cooking was gathered from the woods. It was a community project with some neighbors assisting. Wagons, axes, splitters, and cross-cut saws were used to fell the tall trees, cut them up, and transport the wood home. I just watched. Hay bailing to provide food for the livestock was also done as a community project with neighbors helping. I was allowed to tie the wires that were punched around the bales on the non-mobile hay baler.

Grandpa Cleve Wright raised corn in the field northwest of the house. It was "new" ground, black with humus, and rich. He loved large horses, and used them for the farm work. He would sweat as he put the horses through their paces. On one occasion, a horse collapsed in the harness, as he put it through its paces. He was a large man, and the size matching was appropriate. He loved hard work. As a young man, he had owned good teams to pull the swamp boats with logs out of Mingo. He is shown below with his two sons and brother-in-law in the picture. They were all about six and one-half feet tall.

Men in Wright family. Pictured from left: Worda Wright, Cleve Wright, Carl Harper, and Charles Wright.

The work began early on the farm. After the dusky dawn chores and breakfast, the horses were harnessed, and a plow was attached. Dad Wright would walk in back of the plow, and guide it by hand in a straight furrow from one end of the field to the other. Sometimes he would let me walk behind the plow and guide it. However, there were drawbacks to this activity. Frequently, we plowed up a bed of snakes, and they were scattered all around. In the fall, corn was picked into a wagon, and stored in the corn cribs in the barn. Very few people had tractors at that time, and we traveled with Dad Wright in a wagon pulled by horses to work areas on and near the farm.

In the lowlands of southeast Missouri, the drainage ditches were full and much of the land wooded. I remember going with my father to pick up a couple of pigs that he had purchased. We proceeded east of Dexter on a narrow unpaved road for several miles through a very swampy area. It was near Panther Swamp. Finally, we came upon a clearing on higher ground, and a man came out of a rundown cabin and greeted Dad. They apparently knew each other and were friendly in their meeting. They talked for a while, and then got down to business in discussing the price. Dad cut out the corners of two burlap bags, and the man came around the house carrying a pig. He held it by one ear and by the tail. They stuffed it in one of the bags, tied the end, and placed it in the trunk of the car. Then he brought the other pig, and carried it the same way. How convenient that God had provided handles for carrying the pigs. Dad paid the man, they shook hands, smiled, and we waved goodbye. We hauled the pigs home and turned them loose in the pen. They kind of stood around for a while, but soon were active and no worse for the wear.

Swamps were common back then. My great uncle near Dudley, Missouri, lived on high ground that was not connected to the roadway. To visit him, we had to get into a flat-bottom boat and pole our way out across the bayou to his home. He and his family would rush out to greet us. They didn't have much company. It was a joy to see them, and we visited with them as long as we could. We returned back to the road using the boat, and left it tied up, but unlocked as we had found it.

My Dad's favorite hunting area was near Dudley. I remember

the tall trees and his bringing home numerous squirrels. We needed fresh meat when the pork in the smoke houses was depleted. He taught me how to clean the squirrels. Mom would fry them and serve them with gravy. The meals Mom prepared as a part of the squirrel dinner were delicious. We ate fish as well. The men would make trips to the Mingo Swamp and the drainage ditches, and seine the fish. I knew about catfish when I was four years old.

My Grandpa Shell was also quite a woodsman. When younger, he had surprised a bear in the woods and chased it. He was proud of this and told me the story many times. He did not try to kill it, although he did have a gun with him. He sure was a brave man. He was also very good at finding bee trees. He would spot a bee flying in the woods, and could trace it to its hive in a tree. He also allowed me to watch him take the honey from the hives behind his house. He had a net over his head and his skin was covered. He was never stung, although the bees swarmed over his entire head. There was honey on the table at almost every meal.

Our main meal was at noon, and we called it dinner. We had breakfast in the morning, and supper in the evening. We recycled the food. Any food left over at the end of the day was eaten for supper, and the remaining food-scraps dumped in the slop barrel behind the house to feed the hogs. Dad would mix this slop with whey from the Ozark dairy, and with shorts, and pour it into the hog trough. The pigs would make every meal sound like it was the best they had ever eaten in their lives.

I learned a lot about pigs during those days. If they suddenly stopped eating and started losing weight, Dad would break-up some coal, and throw the lumps into the pen. The pigs would eat the coal, crunching it down. After a day or two, normal eating would return. Occasionally, the pigs would have skin hives. Dad would build supports wrapped with burlap bags, and soaked with cylinder oil. After a day or two of rubbing themselves against the bags, the pigs were cured. Otherwise, they lived a life of luxury until Thanksgiving.

I don't ever remember being hungry during the Depression. The sharing of food among the families and neighbors managed to keep everyone afloat, including the hobos. Only money was in short supply, and we had no pensions or welfare.

Medicine and Cures

One of the most difficult problems before World War II was that there were no antibiotics. People would get sick and could not be helped. Good medical procedures were also very limited in the Dexter area. Either one's genes pulled you through, or one was lost.

My Uncle Paul Sitton got a splinter in his eye while he worked on a roof. It became infected, and he lost his eye. Uncle Arthur Shell was a Baptist minister. The churches were not air-conditioned. One would get hot and sweaty during the services, and cool off later, outside. After exposure to the hot and cold, Uncle Arthur eventually developed either bronchitis or tuberculosis, and after a lingering illness, passed away. He left his wife, Willie Shell, and four children, Eleanora, Gladys, Truman, and Alva.

Uncle Johnson Wiseman developed a stomach ulcer, which became gangrenous. Because of the deficient diet that many had in their early years, stomach problems were very common. My father suffered from a bad stomach his entire life.

The gangrene spread in Uncle Johnson and he died. He left his wife, Alta Wiseman, and two children, Cecil and Lola.

He and Aunt Alta are shown in the picture on the following page. Aunt Alta was very pretty, and looked somewhat like her grandmother, Mary Martindale.

Ironically, penicillin became available about two years later. Whether or not this would have saved Uncle Johnson is not known.

Kerosene was another medicine used in many cases in the early days. If you stepped on a nail, you soaked your foot in kerosene. If you had a bad cough, a little sugar in kerosene was often used, and you swallowed a sip of it. Sometimes turpentine was substituted for kerosene. I was told that kerosene was good for a snake bite, although I never experienced one. Aspirin was the only medicine available for headaches. The oil of wintergreen liniment, a chemical cousin to aspirin, was good for sore muscles. Castor oil was used as a laxative, and paregoric (opium tincture) for diarrhea. Mercurochrome was applied to scratches, and Syrup of Pepsin was good for an upset stomach. Quinine was used for malaria, although I never suffered from it.

Johnson and Alta Wiseman

One disease that could not be helped was polio. It attacked millions of people, including President Roosevelt. It left them crippled, and in some cases killed them.

Doctors could be visited at their offices, or would visit someone at home if he or she was very sick. My father had a car, and would give relatives and neighbors rides to the doctor's office. Some people would pay part of their bills by bartering chickens or similar goods. There was a hospital in Poplar Bluff, but people only went there for very serious illnesses.

My brother Bill and I became very ill one cold winter, and each developed a high fever. The fevers would not break, and aspirin did not help. The whole family was concerned, and it was feared that we had the flu or something worse. We were moved from our cold bedroom onto the couch in the front room. Bill was placed at one end of the couch, and I at the other with our feet touching. The pot bellied stove in the middle of the room kept us warm. We felt bad from the fever, and griped and griped about our toes touching. That went on for a day or two, and Dad was very worried. He went to see Dr. Davis who could not make a house call until the next day. When the Doctor arrived, he could see Dad's anguish, and quickly examined us. He looked long and hard, and said, "Harvey, look at this rash. Your boys have the measles." What a relief for everyone, and the fever broke that very night.

Later, we suffered the mumps and chicken pox, but fared better with them.

When I was about five years old, I had whooping cough. It persisted, and later a secondary infection developed in my eyes. Dad took me to see a specialist, Dr. Hoxie, in Poplar Bluff. His diagnosis was that I had granulated eyelids, and that they needed to be scraped. I was laid on a cot, and they would hold me down while a chloroform mask was forced over my face. The chloroform smothered me, and I fought them until the gas put me to sleep. This must have been like it feels to be smothered to death. The procedure was performed three or four times, and I still have claustrophobia from it. After each procedure, I would wake up the next morning with my eyelids stuck shut, and my mother would have to physically pull them open – and that hurt. I cried and cried. Dad realized that I was not improving, and he took me to visit Dr. Dieckmann in Dexter. The doctor said that my problem was one of nutrition. He recommended that I be put out in the sun as much as possible, even on days when it was a little cold, and that I be given cod liver oil. I immediately became better, and finally my eyes healed. The right one was crossed, however, and I had only partial vision in it for the rest of my life.

In 1943, my Grandpa Shell's appendix ruptured. He was taken to the Poplar Bluff Hospital, but gangrene set in before we got him there. He was very sick. The doctors said that they had a new drug that might help. The family had about given up on his survival, and was very worried. They were willing to try anything to save him. The drug was given. Much to our surprise, he got better, and was well within a short while. That was my first knowledge of penicillin.

Grandpa later developed something that penicillin would not cure. It was a spot on his lip that the doctors called cancer. It was very sore and painful. He had to shave off his mustache. The doctors were able to burn the cancer off with radium.

My Grandpa Shell had a heart malfunction that he called heart dropsy. He would suddenly pass out after only a little exertion. There was no such thing as open-heart surgery or stents to be placed in the arteries. Perhaps he would have lived beyond his seventy-nine years if he had lived today. He had good genes.

Works Progress Administration (WPA)

In the late 1930s, our street was invaded by hundreds of people working under a program that was a part of President Roosevelt's New Deal. They called it the Works Progress Administration, or WPA. The government was trying to employ as many people as possible to mitigate the impact of the Great Depression. An overlap on the jobs occurred, and left many standing around. Some people said that WPA stood for "We Piddle Around."

Bill and Sevia Shell

Uncle Bill Shell worked for the WPA. He was a small man and had very little education. He had a wife, Aunt Sevia, and four children, and worked at any job that he could find. Jobs were scarce.

His job with the WPA was a life saver for the family. Cash was essential, even though gardens and food were available.

The WPA built a sidewalk along our side of the street, and built some modern style sanitary (outdoor) toilets. I remember everyone going to view Grandpa Shell's new WPA outdoor toilet, and wishing that they had one like it. The base of it was made of concrete, including the stool.

Uncle Bill was involved in those WPA projects as well as others. He provided janitorial cleaning at the schools as a part of his job. He also supported the school lunch programs. He helped to plant, harvest, and preserve the produce for the school lunch programs. He also assisted in cooking the food.

In the picture below, the Bill Shell children are posing in their front yard. The road behind them is the Old Bloomfield Road, and across the road to the east is the Dexter Cemetery (south end). Notice that the road is an unpaved gravel road.

Uncle Bill was very thankful for his WPA job, and worked hard to keep it. He never had time to stand around or piddle around in his job. The family was very proud that President Roosevelt had created the WPA.

The Bill Shell Family: Faustina, Beauton, Imogene, and Eugene

The WPA workers were always around, several of them. At the time, it seemed like a waste, but they did build a lasting infrastructure and contributed to improving the depressed economy. Dad did not want to admit that anything had improved. My father was a strong Republican, and one of only a few in Dexter, or in all of Southeast Missouri for that matter.

Uncle Bill was also a strong republican, but his WPA experiences had given him a different opinion, and he was right.

I saw the WPA people everywhere. At noon at our grocery store, they ate crackers, cheese and bologna. Typically, they would also have a bottle of milk. I never went to the store without getting hungry from just listening to them chew. To this day, I still like that kind of fare, and feel secure when I eat it.

The Hubbard & Goforth Grocery where we shopped was in the Cotton Belt. It was located at the southeast corner of the intersection of Highway 60 and Stoddard Street. It was much like the one I imagined from the radio series, "Lum & Abner's Jot'M' Down Store and Library." The two proprietors, Hubbard & Goforth, were there in the store everyday. A long flat counter was in the front side of the store, and a large cash register was in the middle. Canned groceries lined the shelves behind the counter, followed by bags of coffee, flour, and sugar. A wall-mounted telephone was by the front door. Two large glass windows were in the front. We bought all of our groceries on a credit account that we paid monthly. A potbellied stove was in the back of the store, and there was room for people to eat, mill around, play checkers, and talk. They could help themselves to the cracker barrel, and cheese, and there was a cooler with chunks of ice for milk and sodas. The milk was in glass bottles with cardboard caps to seal them, and the soda came in bottles. The soda bottles came in various sizes, and my favorite was Pepsi Cola. I liked it because it came in the largest size. Each patron would keep account of what they purchased for lunch, and pay for the food before they left. Kerosene was in a horizontal barrel in the very back. The clothes, gloves, soap, and tools were on the other side of the store.

Many times I would walk from our home in Old Dexter down the hill to the Cotton Belt, buy groceries, and walk back up the hill with my arms full. It was on this hill that my Grandpa Shell had one of his heart dropsy attacks. It was painless. He just fell, rolled over, caught his breath, got up and proceeded up the hill.

Hubbard and Goforth were talkers, and about every subject in the world came up during the course of a day. The world in 1939 through 1941 had a broad base of subjects. The WPA workers carried in many of the stories. Much of the news was local, but discussions about the possibility of war, the economy, the Joe Louis heavyweight fights, or baseball games were regular. Sometimes a singer or other type of entertainer would stand outside the entrance and do his thing. One time we had a ventriloquist, reeking of whiskey, displaying a little talking dummy. I was very much impressed, and tried unsuccessfully for a long time to "throw" my voice.

Activities along my street during that time included the postman delivering mail to street-side mailboxes, and the iceman hauling ice in a horse-drawn wagon. We would run along after the wagon, and get chips of ice to suck on, as he lifted blocks of ice with his tongs and carried them to the houses. Refrigerators were not yet available. The ice went into insulated iceboxes. A sign in the window told the iceman whether to deliver ice that day. Sometimes people would buy ice directly off the wagon. A piece of twine was tied around the block of ice, and they would carry it by the twine to their home.

Sometimes people came by selling services. I remember a photographer coming by with a large box camera on a tripod. He led a Shetland pony that people could sit on for pictures. We didn't have a picture taken since we couldn't afford it, but I did like his pony, and hung around it closely for awhile.

Not all of the unemployed worked for the WPA. Some of the younger men joined the Civilian Conservation Corps (CCC). They were assigned to the various public projects throughout the state such as construction at Big Springs and Alley Springs State Parks. The layout and organization of those projects was done by the CCC boys, and they did a very good job. Many of those young men would later enter the armed services.

Daily Family Activities

We had chores to do to earn an allowance. I would fill up the coal bucket each day in the winter, and my brother would cut the kindling. Dad would close the damper on the potbellied stove and bank the ashes before we went to bed. The damper was a levered vent at the bottom of the stove where the air intake could be adjusted. When the damper was wide open, the fire burned profusely, and the stove would get rosy hot. At night, Dad closed it for safety purposes, and covered the hot coals with dry ashes.

There was always the possibility of having fires in the flue. The ashes had to be taken out each day, and a container in the bottom of the stove was removed and taken outside and dumped. Sometimes that lot fell on my shoulders.

My father had rigged up suspenders on my bedding to hold it down. My brother and I shared the bed. We slept on a thick featherbed with quilts on top. We would sink into the feather bed until most of our bodies were submerged. When the alarm clock sounded in the morning, I would hear my dad's bare feet hit the floor, and hear them thumping in a run to the front room. He would open the damper on the stove, stir the coals from the night before, and add kindling. He would then pour in kerosene, and the flames would blast up. Then he dumped coal into the stove, and Dad would run back to the bed and cover up. Soon there was a red-hot stove, and the family would come alive. The ice on the water bucket would be broken, and that ice which was solid in the wash pan, was dumped out the back door. Dad would heat water in the wash pan, and generate some lather in a soap mug. He would then apply it to his face, and shave with a flat blade in his safety razor. The blade was sharp along one side, and would last for a couple of shaves.

My Grandpa Shell used a long straight razor that he sharpened with a leather razor strap before each use. It was rumored that the strap could also be used for spanking. My mother would cook breakfast, and the day proceeded.

The Christmas celebrations were very exciting. Santa first came to our house when I was about five. My brother and cousin, Louis Henry Cook, were just crawling. We were all gathered in the living room, and there was a knock at the door. Dad had hired a Santa who had plenty of antifreeze in his tank. He came in laughing loudly with a bag of toys, and started handing them out. He had all types of windup toys, motorcycles, noisemakers, and others, and set them in motion. The toddlers just crawled around with their eyes wide open. I got to talk to Santa. It was warm and cozy and the potbellied stove did its part.

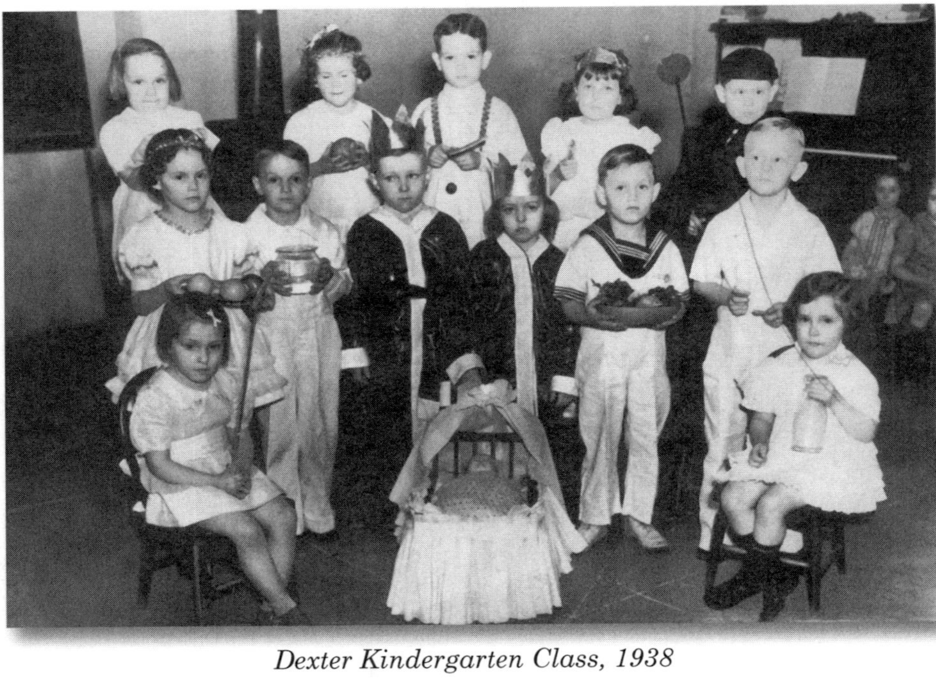

Dexter Kindergarten Class, 1938

Top row: Peggy Jo Eagle, Doris Jean Miller, Scott Jones, Vivian Allen, Harvey Shell. Next row: Unknown, Charles Worley, Ronald Mouser, Marlene Wagner, Unknown, Jimmy Lemons. Next row: Unknowns.

Later school entered the picture. I would get dressed in overalls, sometimes with patched knees, and head for school. My early days were rough. I had daily comments from some about my crossed eyes, but with time, the situation got better. On the previous page is a picture of my kindergarten class. Note that I was the little black goblin with the crossed eyes. My cousin Ronald Mouser was the king in the middle.

There were two first grade and second grade classes. The rest were single classes, until the sixth grade was reached and the classes rotated from room to room by subject matter.

The principal was rumored to have a spanking machine in his office, but I could not verify its existence. Several boys said that they had experienced it.

The early school years were uneventful. One big problem occurred in the first grade, and I thought for sure that the paddling machine would be put into action. Several of the young boys had hung around after school, and walked on the desks with mud on their shoes. They even jumped from desk to desk. They got into big, big trouble. My cousin Ronald Mouser was involved with that bunch, but not me. However, much to my disappointment, the spanking machine was not put into action.

In the "Rhyme of the Ancient Mariner" by Samuel Taylor Coleridge, the mariner had killed an albatross while at sea, causing a curse to be invoked upon his entire ship. The crew tied the dead albatross to the mariner's neck to remind him of the bad luck he had caused. After several years, the bird fell from his neck and the curse was lifted. My albatross was the Principal's spanking machine. It was a constant concern of mine. My Aunt Lovie Webb told me during the sixth grade that the machine didn't exist. She was a school teacher, and could speak with authority. I believed her. The albatross dropped from my neck, and I became much more daring in my lifestyle.

During the first and second grades, my mother would pack the most delicious luncheon meals for me, and I enjoyed them very much. And in the fall, we had taffy pulls, apple dunking, and popcorn balls, and would sing the songs of the season. We pressed leaves and coated them with paraffin, and did all kinds of neat things with paper.

I always looked forward to the music class. The classroom was downstairs near the dining room. The teacher would say, "Now don't run, or push while going down the stairs." We would rush down the stairs at the speed of light before she could even get to the entrance to observe. Everyone would then stand and say the Pledge of Allegiance. At that time, "Under God" was not a part of it. We then sang "My Country Tis' of Thee" and other patriotic songs, and then got down to business. One of my favorites was "I've been working on the railroad." Another was "Solomon Levi" (my name is Solomon Levi / my store's on Salem Street / that's where you can buy your coats and hats / and everything that's neat / Second handed underwear / and overcoats so fine / for all the boys who trade with me / one hundred and forty nine / O' Solomon Levi, la, la, la, la, la, la - O' Solomon Levi, la, la, la, la, la, la ----).

We sang all the Steven Foster songs. My favorites were "Jeanie With the Light Brown Hair," "Carry Me Back to Old Virginia" and "Old Black Joe." Songs of the seasons were also promoted at Thanksgiving, Christmas, and Easter.

During all of this time, the cooks in the kitchen down the hall were cooking their best fare. We had spent an eternity smelling the savory fare. I remember stew, and sauerkraut and wieners being on some of their menus, and as soon as music class was over, we hurried to the lunchroom for food.

After lunch was over, the playground waited. We played marbles, tag, rode on the merry-go-round, played in the swings or rode the see-saw. The girls also played jacks and hop scotch. Softball was a big sport for both boys and girls. When the bell rang, we would come in covered with dust and sweat, and no one seemed to mind. After school we could wash it all off in a wash pan filled with soapy water.

Reading was a wonderful part of school. We had a grade school library, and I read every book that I could get my hands on. My early books and series included those by Zane Grey (Western Novels), Samuel Clemens *Tom Sawyer*, Robert Louis Stevenson *Treasure Island*, and Laura Lee Hope *The Bobbsey Twins*. The reading later included books and stories by Nathaniel Hawthorne *Various*, Herman Melville *Moby Dick*, James Oliver Curwood *Nature Adventure*

Books, Pearl Buck *The Good Earth*, Harriet Beecher Stowe *Uncle Tom's Cabin*, John Steinbeck *Grapes of Wrath*, and even Margaret Mitchell's *Gone with the Wind*, not bad for grade school reading. I liked them all, but perhaps liked the stories by Hawthorne, Clemens, and Curwood the best.

Entertainment

My Aunt Mary Sitton was the only one on our street with a phone. It was wall mounted, and was on a party line. We did not have a telephone until after 1945. When we picked up the receiver, the operator answered with "number please." We answered with a three-digit number. For instance, the number for City Motor Sales (now Bud Shell Ford) was 337.

Airplanes were used in the 1930s. Mail planes flew over our house once or twice per day, and were so high we could hardly see them. I understood at the time that they were flying between St. Louis and Memphis. One big treat was when an old WWI biplane took a nose dive at me and my friends while we were playing.

The daily newspaper that we subscribed to was the *Daily American Republic*, published in Poplar Bluff, Missouri. I remember that I learned to read the cartoons section while in the first grade. "Alley Oop," "Dick Tracy," "Red Ryder," "Superman," "Flash Gordon," and "Freckles and his Friends" were my favorites. I started reading those when the first comic series about Santa Claus appeared. Later, I started reading the news.

When I first came home from school, I would play with my friends, do my chores, and read the paper. Then after supper, I would prop my feet up on the rim on the pot bellied stove and listen to the radio. The whole family would gather and listen to the stories. There were different stories each night; "Lum and Abner," "Amos and Andy," "Sky King," "Sergeant Preston of the Yukon," "Henry Aldridge," "The Lone Ranger," "Fibber McGee and Molly," "Jack

Benny," "Red Skelton" and "Edgar Bergen and Charlie McCarthy" are examples. They allowed us to use our imagination to the limit.

On Friday night, I went to the movies with my mother and father. We watched movies with actors like Lassie, Gary Cooper, John Wayne, Humphrey Bogart, Clark Gable, Errol Flynn, Randolph Scott, Judy Garland, Mickey Rooney, Betty Davis, Ingrid Bergen, Kathryn Hepburn, Bert Lahr, Stan Laurel, Oliver Hardy, Bela Lugosi, Joan Crawford, Jean Harlow, and many, many, others. The "Boston Blackie," "Sherlock Holmes," and "Thin Man" series were also well liked.

Every Saturday afternoon, the family went to town. They visited with relatives, shopped, paid bills, and in the case of my Grandpa Wright, took the eggs and cream to sell. Some of the stores along Main Street in Dexter included Citizens Bank, Graber's, Gainers Jewelry, Throwers Men's Store, Parker's Drug Store, Weber's, Stovall's, Ike Smith's Grocery, Allen's Barber Shop, Ringer Hardware, Sisler's, Morgan Furniture Company, and Weeks Theater. The Citizens Bank was on the corner. Sigler Chevrolet was one block south of it, and to the north was Crane's Service Station, the Railroad Depot, and Riddle's Lumber Company. Further east down the railroad track near the shirt factory was a streetcar that had been imported and made into a restaurant. Dexter was a quiet, friendly little town with agricultural surroundings. Everyone knew each other.

While the adults did their thing, the kids went to the movies, and watched the cowboy shows, which took all afternoon. Gene Autry, Roy Rogers, and Tex Ritter were my heroes, and in addition to the movies, cartoons, and short serial features were shown. The serial sequence would always end with the heroes appearing to be to be in utmost danger, and facing almost certain death. We would return the next Saturday to find that they had miraculously survived, but by the end of this episode they were in another cliff-hanger. By that time, we were tired and ready to go home.

After I got a little older, I spent every moment playing cowboy. My two older cousins, Cecil Wiseman, and Eugene Shell, joined me with other friends. We would run, hide, jump out, and make gunshot sounds as we surprised each other.

Cecil Wiseman and Lola Wiseman

Faustina, Imogene and Eugene Shell

Cecil Wiseman and Eugene Shell were young and still in training as cowboys in the pictures above.

We would act out the movies and books. The action in most cases was a game of chase, hide out, and shoot. Sometimes, I would ride a broomstick horse. I remember riding my stick horse down the Old Dexter hill where smoking embers from burned weeds still smoldered. I sang, "As I Rode the Navajo Trail," and "Don't Fence Me In." The smell of the smoke made it very realistic. I had a Gene Autry cap pistol with pearl handles. On rare occasions, someone had a box of caps, and that made the play more realistic with the loud pops and clatter. Unfortunately, a box of caps would only last an hour or two. Anyway, there was ample time for me to learn how to become a seasoned cowboy.

The spring season ended with many activities. On May 1, going "bare-footed" was allowed, and swimming was allowed on May 15. At least, that is what we children believed was true, and our demands would persist until the Adults gave in. The fashion for the summer was for the kids to go without shoes.

May 1, (May Day) was a holiday for the schools. Poles were erected, and the day was celebrated. Generally, four or five May Poles were placed on the football field, next to the original Dexter High School. The grade school and high school kids were dressed in their best. They carried colored paper streamers and interwove them around the poles.

They circled the poles, braiding the paper as they alternately passed each other, and sang throughout the activity. The interweaving proceeded until the multicolored streamers were woven all the way down to the bottom of the poles.

Lightning bugs appeared, and we could spend about a month catching them. We could never catch enough to light up the neighborhood.

June bugs appeared about the time the lightning bugs were gone. They were large, round bugs, green in color, and were excellent fish bait. We would sometimes tie threads to their legs, and hold on. They would fly around and around us until their energy was gone. It was great fun, and was certainly an improvement over playing marbles at school during an endless spring.

There was an abundance of children in "Old Dexter" with whom to play and share ideas. The people in my age class included Marian and Charles Sitton, Coreene Sitton, Wanda Lee Lane and Dale Lane, Jimmy Baker, Pauline Eskew and Deloris Eskew, Leon Corlew and Buddy Corlew, Patsy Shell and Clifford Shell, Charles Vanbibber, Billy Hutchraft, Betty Jo Wright, Cecil Wiseman, Eugene Shell, Richard Wilcox, Dwight Williams and Duane Williams, Tony Landers, Pansy Carwile, and my brother, Bill.

Ronald Mouser from across town frequently joined us. Virginia Mouser visited us several times from St. Louis, and lived in Dexter for awhile. Some of those we played with are shown in the pictures.

Virginia Mouser

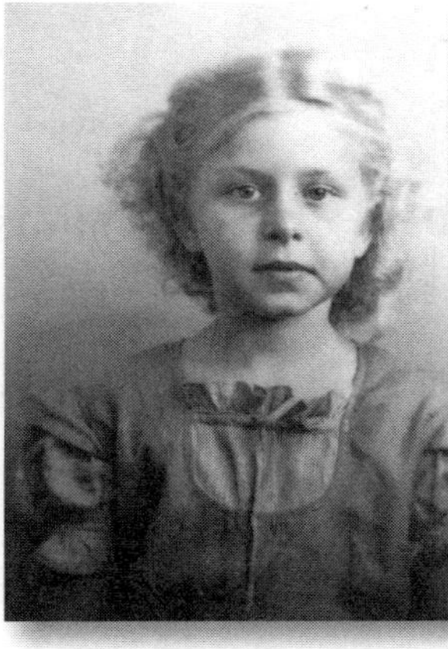

Phyllis Shell

Patsy Shell

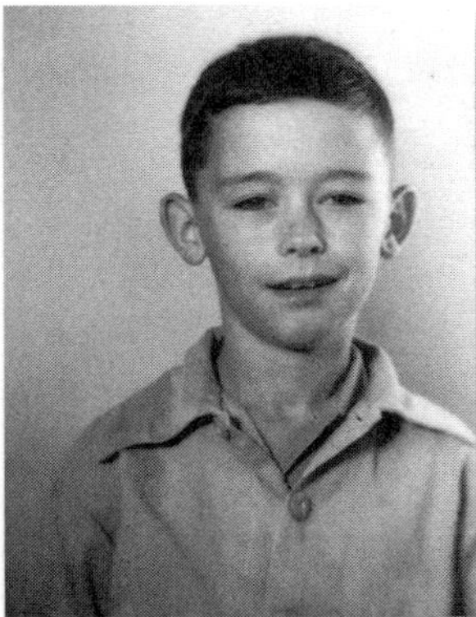

Charles VanBibber

Dwight Williams

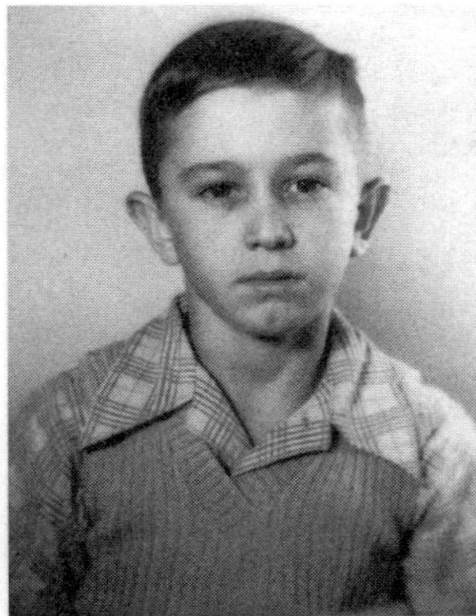

Clifford "Bud" Shell

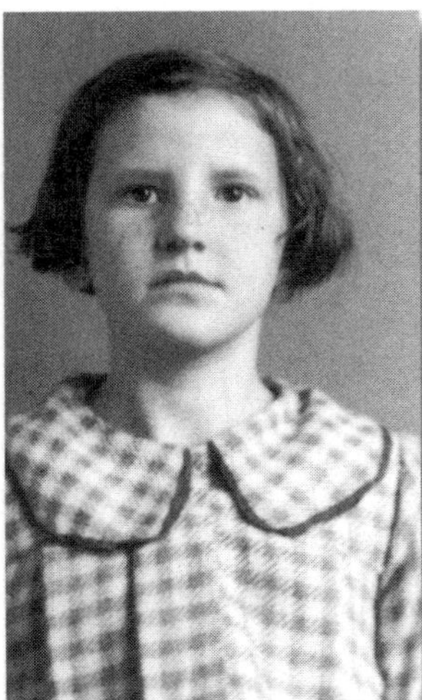

Betty Wright

Ronald, Jerry and Beverly Wright

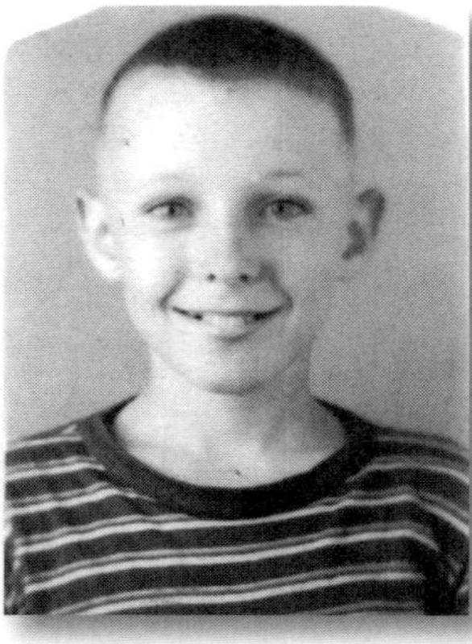

Ronald Mouser

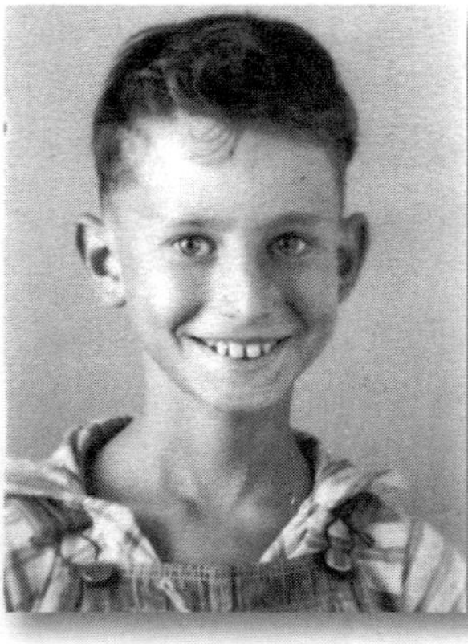

Donald Rose

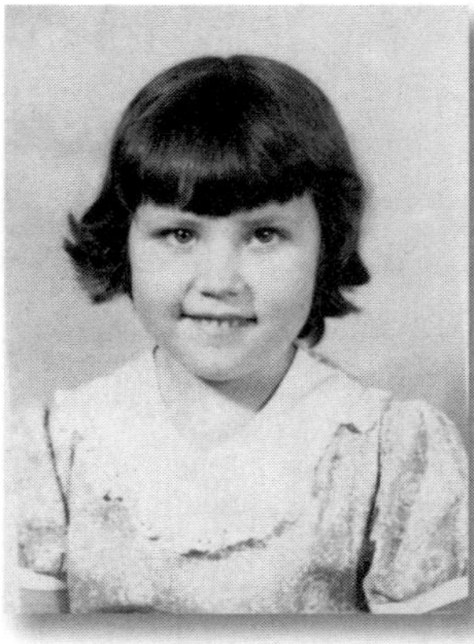

Ellen Sitton

Joyce Sitton

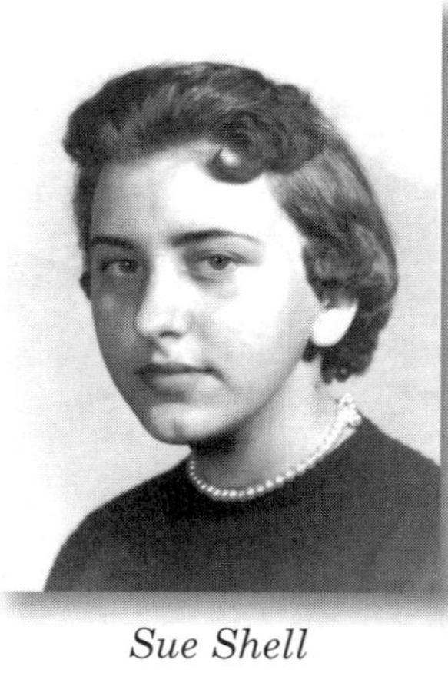

Sue Shell

Charles and Marian Sitton

Viewing our world. Pictured from left: Cousin Charles Sitton, Cousin Marian Sitton, Coreene Sitton, Cousin Lewis Cook, Harvey Shell, Bill Shell, and Cousin Logan Cook.

In addition to softball, war and cowboys and Indians, we played "Hide and Go Seek," Tag, Pitching Horseshoes, Checkers, and "Red Rover, Red Rover." We climbed trees, and played in the hay in barns. The girls played house, hopscotch, jumped rope, and tossed jacks, and the boys played with cars and trucks.

Lewis and Logan Cook were great fun, and were daring. One time they were found under their house with matches and newspapers. It was too damp for anything to start burning, but they tried hard. They sometimes visited school with my brother and me, and kept our classmates excited. Logan was especially active, eating paste, drinking ink, and throwing paper wads.

We finally got electricity along our entire street, and had streetlights to play under. We would scatter boards and other materials to mark the bases, and play softball on the gravel road. Both boys and girls would participate, and the few cars that came by stopped while we cleared the field. The streetlights also added support when we gathered together to tell ghost stories. I was almost too scared when we disbanded, and I had to walk home through the dark to my house. I dreamed that I saw a ghost one time under the house. It looked like a polar bear.

Special Events

There were always things going on in Dexter. The Fall Festival was one of my favorites with carnival rides and shows. It was held in the Cotton Belt on the vacant airport land, and the whole town attended. It was celebrated in late September, and the nights were cool. I remember that Dad talked my mother into attending a dancing girl show that he wanted to attend in one of the tents. He found that she was not too fond of the girls in the show kicking their legs up, and we left it in a hurry. I didn't find it too offensive, however.

Other tents went up in the summer. Some were on the vacant Armory lot. There were singing conventions, medicine shows, and church revivals. Sometimes a wrestler would come to town and announce that he could whip anyone in Dexter. A hero would show up and take him on. Everyone said that the fights were always fixed.

One time, the Nashville stars of the Grand Ole Opry showed up. Bill Monroe, Earnest Tubbs, and Roy Acuff were among the celebrities. I swore after that show that I would be a hillbilly singer, and my favorite singer was Bill Monroe. Dad later bought me a second-hand potato bug mandolin, and I learned to play it by ear. My Grandpa Shell later showed me off in front of my cousin Alva Shell and his band, and they donated money for my books and training. They had a great band. I was on my way to a glorious future. Alas, my only important achievement was to play occasional songs at church.

One event that was especially interesting was the visit of Robert Wadlo. He was from Alton, Illinois. His height was 8 feet 11

1/2 inches tall. An area was roped off on Main Street in Dexter. He challenged everyone for a fee to reach up and retrieve a $100 bill from the top of his head. My Uncle Worda Wright excitedly made a try, but failed.

In fact, everyone in the crowd that had lined up and tried also failed. Mr. Wadlo finally left town with his $100 bill and all the fees. It was the talk of the town for several days after it had occurred. The Wright family had several tall members, and my Uncle Charlie Wright was the tallest. Unfortunately, he was not present at the event. Everyone in the family speculated that he would have accomplished it, and we sure did need the money. However, with time, we finally stopped crying over sour grapes.

We attended the Nazarene Church in the Cotton Belt, and were loyal members. Brother A.C. Roland was the Pastor, and his children were the ages of my brother and me. The church services were warm and alive. My aunt Alta Wiseman was a shouter, and an inspiration to all, and people came down to the mourner's bench every night for prayer. We had a testimonial service at the end of every service. The kids learned to say, "I am saved and sanctified, and on my way to heaven," and we meant it. The church was the backbone of our community during the War.

The church was full every Sunday. The people got the cardboard hand fans out of the racks behind the pews, and waved them in front of their faces during the summer to keep themselves cool. Women nursed their babies in church, generally in the back, but not always.

We kids kept busy. A retired preacher, Brother Churchill, played a base drum during the music services, accompanied by several of us kids on our instruments – me with my mandolin. Coreene Sitton and I sang, "Lily of the Valley" one night to a standing ovation. That boosted my ego tremendously.

After communion one night, the pastor's son and I were wandering in the church basement, and ran across the leftover grape juice. We helped ourselves to it. No need to let it spoil.

Someone set up a revival tent in the summer on an empty lot near the church, and it was filled to capacity every night. One girl said that she loved those revivals, and got saved every year.

I sometimes had fear as I walked home from church afterward. I could imagine that the sky was lighting up, and the world was coming to an end. One night, I dreamed that I was in front of church, and that my feet kept sinking into the ground.

Well, church does keep one honest and on his toes, and I needed that. When I was seven, I had my first experience with sin. My cousin, Ronald Mouser, from the new part (elite and decadent part) of Dexter came to see me, and told me that he had learned some cuss words. He wanted to practice them. We climbed on top of my Grandpa Shell's chicken house, and shouted the PG rated words as loud as we could. We jumped up and down, and yelled and yelled and yelled, and finally tired of the exercise. No one heard us yelling except God. My cousin told me not to tell anyone, and I didn't.

It was also at this age that I had my first artistic experience of drawing nude females. My friend told me that there was nothing to it. "Just draw a figure eight, and add the necessary features." I did as he said, and prepared the drawing. I was satisfied with the results, and felt no guilt.

He then said, "We are really in trouble!!" I said, "We are?" That came as a complete shock to me, and I was very afraid and upset. We took the paper deep into the weeds behind my house and threw it away. A day or two later, my cousin confronted me with the drawing. He said that he had found it in the weeds, and asked if I drew it. I said, "Yes, I did." He said, "You are really in trouble, if your Dad finds out." He agreed to take the drawing and destroy it.

Some years later, I read the story, "The Minister's Black Veil," by Nathaniel Hawthorne. The preacher said that he had committed sins that were too dark to confess to people on earth. His sins were hidden under his black veil. My sinful activities were the start of my black veil. It has grown larger and larger ever since.

We visited with both sets of our grandparents on a regular basis. Bill and I spent the night with them fairly often. Occasionally, my cousin, Ronald Mouser, joined us at Grandpa Shell's. We would wrestle, play, and stay up until the wee hours. Bill would go to sleep early, and Ronald and I would carry on. Grandpa Shell would turn the lights out. It was black in the house. He would yell at us from time to time. Finally, Ronald would go to sleep. Grandpa had a large upright clock that clicked very loud, and would gong from time to time. It kept me awake, and was scary, but I survived. The frequency of the trips to each of our grandparent's homes was at least once per week.

It was always a treat to visit Grandpa Shell. The home was cozy, and my two aunts kept life friendly. With Grandma Shell, it meant that there were three women competing with one man. Sometimes grandpa would get enough and not talk to any of them. Aunt Dora accused him of pouting. That agitated him still more.

Aunt Dora would always make me a separate little pie, when she made a full pie for the family. There was no spoiling going on despite comments from some of the family. Grandpa called me his boy, and Grandma called my Brother her boy. We accepted those titles with joy. One time Grandpa scooped some soap suds from a wash tub, and showered them all over my brother. Bill said, "If you want to 'trow' suds on someone, 'trow' them on your own boy."

We enjoyed dinners with the family members often at both of our grandparents' homes, especially during good weather. Dinners always took place during the summer when the Uncle Zeno Wright family from Ruston, Louisiana and the Uncle George Harper family from San Diego, California would visit.

A dinner at the Harper/Wright family reunion is shown in the picture below.

Mary Harper McMillon, a cousin, is standing with her back to the camera. My mother is in the gray dress on the left side of the table. I am across from her

Harper/Wright Family Reunion

on the right side. The table is unique. Wooden sawhorses topped with boards usually made the table, which then was covered with tablecloths. In this case, the table had legs made of concrete blocks. After use, the tables could be dismantled and put in the shed. The dinners were not a sit down affair. The people sat on the ground or in some chairs from the house and used their laps as tables.

The dinners were held in the yard under shade trees. Everyone brought vegetables of different kinds, and several pies and deserts – always in great abundance. Pork, chicken and dumplings, biscuits, and salads were always furnished. Tea, orange, and grape drink were contained in large clay pots with a chunk of ice in the middle. And, there was coffee.

The event below was very special, and was enjoyed by everyone. Grandpa Shell was 75 years old.

Grandpa Shell's 75th Birthday Party
Lorena Shell and Grandpa Shell

Ninety-one people joined in the feast and enjoyed good eats of all kinds. Over one hundred people visited the home. Three specially-baked birthday cakes were presented to Grandpa. In the picture, he is holding two of the cakes in his arms, and Grandma is holding one.

At Dad Wright's Aquilla farm, we attended the ice cream socials and services the Philadelphia Church. I observed my Aunt Betty Jo Wright's baptismal service at Aquilla. It was held in Castor River. Everyone held hands with the preacher leading the procession.

The members stretched about halfway across the river. Everyone started singing, "We Shall Gather At The River," and the minister started baptizing them one-by-one. It was a special service, and reminds me that some things were done better in the old days.

The radio at the Aquilla farm was battery powered, and ran out of power very quickly. We listened to the Lone Ranger every evening, and relished every episode. Dad Wright, and sometimes Mom and and Betty Jo joined us. However, on some occasions the volume would fade in and out until finally the battery was dead. We just sat for a while, and looked at each other.

We made two family vacation trips before WWII. Gasoline was rationed during the War, and none was available for traveling. In 1937, we went to visit our Uncle Zeno Wright in Ruston, Louisiana. A caravan of two 1935 Ford coupes left Southeast Missouri. We had planned on camping on the way since only a few motels were available, and there were several of us on the trip. My mother and father and Dad Wright rode in one coupe. Noah and Lovie Webb and Mom Wright rode in the other, with Charlie Wright riding in the rumble seat. There were no back seats. Betty Jo and I occupied the spaces under the windows behind the front seat of each car.

We could not sit up, but had to lie down for the entire trip. Bill Shell had not yet joined the family. During part of the trip, I was crying. They told me to be quiet, "Betty Jo isn't crying," I said. "But, she doesn't have a sore toe." They checked, and sure enough, I had a reason for crying.

We traveled down the road in the dust with the windows down to keep cool. We wound up after dark in Arkansas, and pulled off the road to camp. There were pine trees, and the needles underneath made great soft beds. After cooking dinner and eating, we went to bed – although we had noticed the mosquitoes. Those critters then came in such swarms, and almost lifted us up out of our beds. We had to pack up and leave. It took us the rest of the night to drive on to Louisiana.

I was young, but I can remember Uncle Zeno's Store. He had giant jars of hard candy and he told me that I could have all I wanted. What wonderful news. I did my best to live out my fondest dream.

In the summer of 1941, we visited Ruston, Louisiana, again with the family. Uncle Zeno's store was much the same as before, but I was a lot more experienced in eating candy.

Other things of interest to me were the stories about alligators in the swamps around Ruston. Uncle Zeno also had a watermelon farm, which was abounding in watermelons. He would only allow us to eat the heart of the watermelon, and would not let us eat it down to the rind.

We left Ruston and drove to Pensacola, Florida, looking for possible work. We had a larger car that time, a 1939 Ford sedan. Dad and Mom Wright, and Betty Jo also made the trip. We parked on the side of the road. There was a small embankment. When we climbed over the embankment, there was nothing but sandy beach and water as far as we could see. It was quite impressive, and almost like viewing a picture.

Pensacola was not too appealing, and we crossed back to Alabama. On the way home from Pensacola, we stayed at a fishing village just across the bay from Biloxi, Mississippi. We could see the lights of Biloxi at night. The fishing camp was made of rather primitive single cabins containing two beds each. That was quite a trip in those days. Most of the people whom we knew then had not even left Southeast Missouri.

There was a long walkway out into the Gulf. We went swimming in the ocean and had a great time. My brother Bill had joined us on the trip. The waves would knock our feet out from under us, as Dad held our hands. Nothing in the job market was forthcoming. During our trip home, between Sikeston and Dexter, a two-winged WWI type plane had crashed and killed the pilot. Someone said he drank a lot, even while flying the plane.

World War II

In a prelude to war, there was a certain excitement in the air brought on by radio broadcasts, newsreels, and our nightly newspaper. It had started especially in 1940 when President Roosevelt had established the military draft. Other events and discussions contributed. Many turned out for a military burial at the Dexter Cemetery. The soldier had died of yellow fever in Panama. Taps were played and repeatedly echoed from several points in the cemetery. This was followed by a rifle salute, and words and prayer were offered at the tomb. This was a very moving ceremony, and even at my young age I could sense the loss.

We were visiting Mom and Dad Wright at the farm on December 7, 1941. I was 8 years old, and would be 9 in three months. Someone came in and excitedly said to turn on the radio. There was a continual broadcast about the Japanese bombing Pearl Harbor. There were repeated recorded statements from President Roosevelt announcing the attack, and declaring war on Japan. That is all that everyone talked about for the rest of the day. My uncle Worda Wright was working in Michigan. He had already received a registration draft notice. Within two weeks he was back at home, and within days was inducted into the Army. His first assignment was Hawaii. That was quite alarming to the family. As it turned out, he served with the military police in Hawaii for the entire duration of the war.

I didn't even know where Pearl Harbor was, or, for that matter, where Hawaii was located. I soon learned as I listened to the conversation. Some said the war wouldn't amount to much. Japan was small and didn't pose much of a problem. We would whip them in less than six months. Betty Jo informed me about a bomb. It was like a large firecracker, made a lot of smoke, and killed people. I had a lot to learn.

Everyone had much to learn. The war changed life the way we had known it. We were in the midst of a great change. The slow-going life of the Depression days had passed, and everyone was in constant motion. Housewives took jobs away from home. Men, husbands and sons were torn away from their families and were cast away to places we had never heard of. The old ways, and many people would be lost forever, and like the lost Lenore in Edgar Allen Poe's poem, "The Raven," they would return nevermore.

I can imagine a similar change in the Shawnee Indians' lifestyle as they had previously departed the land northwest of Bloomfield. Part of the land that they inhabited was on the hill west of Dad Wright's farm, above the swampy land to the north. Arrowheads, pots, tomahawks, fire starters, and water vessels testified to their activities. They were bothered less by mosquitoes and malaria on the hill. Many large swamp rabbits, and other game and fish in Castor River must have kept their larders full. Suddenly, the settlers entered the picture in such great numbers that the Shawnees were forced to leave – and would nevermore return to their previous life.

From the start of the war, people were coming and going. Many were hastily married, expecting separation. Blue stars on placards were in windows throughout the town indicating that young men and women from those homes were serving. Many homes had multiple stars. Some of the stars were silver or gold, indicating that their sons were missing, or would not be coming back. Sometimes, there were multiple silver and gold stars. There was an inner urge from the very beginning for the war to be over. Most of the men were drafted, if physically fit. Some of the farmers and older men were deferred.

We thought that my father would be called. Those with children, and who would be thirty-seven years old by 1943 were exempted. Dad would be only thirty-six years old. We waited and cried, as he left Bloomfield for Jefferson Barracks in St. Louis to take his physical. Except for some rheumatism, he passed the physical without any major problem, and we thought he was gone for sure. The draft board exempted him, probably because he had two children.

Worda Wright was called at the very beginning. Later, my cousins Alva Shell, and Cecil Wiseman were called into the army, and my cousin Beauton Shell joined the Navy "Waves" and served for about three years. These pictures show my cousins in their uniforms. The picture of Worda Wright standing by a jeep was taken in Hawaii. A similar picture is hanging in the Museum at Pearl Harbor. It may be him.

Beauton Shell had taken a job with an automobile company in Michigan, before joining the Waves. When the War was over, she returned to Michigan, and never returned to Crowley's Ridge.

The blue star posted in the window beside Alva Shell indicates that someone (Alva) was serving in the armed services.

Worda Wright

Beauton Shell

Cecil Wiseman

Alva Shell and Sister Gladys Elledge

Vera and Jack Bagby

My Aunt Amanda's son, Bob Shell, served in the Pacific as a marine, and fought in many of the island battles.

Many other relatives and friends served. John Dale Baker, a friend of a girl in the neighborhood, was lost as a tail gunner from a B-17 Flying Fortress, and Jay Crane, a young married man who lived next door was lost in combat. Both young Baker and Crane were first "missing in action."

Jay Crane and his wife were only a couple of kids when he was drafted. They had water fights with my brother and me. They had a baby duck and chicken that they gave us when Jay left. He was never to return. We missed all of the boys very much, and flocked into the churches to offer prayers.

My wife's Uncle Jack Bagby shown in the picture was lost in a submarine in the South China Sea. He was missing in action, and never came back. He was newly married, and left a wife. They had love and the dreams that would never be fulfilled.

I really did not fathom the impact of war, or even the separations that war brought. It was ten years later, after I was drafted during the Korean Conflict that I could understand how it feels being separated from your loved ones and bride.

For me, war was a big adventure. The earlier the Nazis or Japanese invaded Dexter, the more exciting it would be. I expected that to happen very shortly. German submarines off of the East Coast sank several moored ships that had been outlined by the lights on the shore. Japanese shells were fired onto the West Coast. German spies were arrested within the US for planning sabotage, and some were executed.

My dad was an Air Raid Warden, and had a helmet and other gear to wear. He would meet with others, and make response plans for possible attacks. The people in Dexter had heavy blackout blinds over their windows, and would close them during air raid drills. The Dexter fire whistle was used as the air raid siren. When it would sound at night, the blinds had to be closed. Air Raid Wardens were dispatched throughout the city. If a light were spotted, the house was visited and the light covered.

We finally did have a raid, and "bombs" were dropped throughout the city. Dad took me with him the next day to assess the damage. We finally found where a bomb had dropped. It turned out to be a flour bag, and the ground was white. Someone had thrown it on the ground in simulation. Boy, was I disappointed. I thought it would have been a real bomb, and would have been dropped from an airplane.

By the beginning of the War, we had a sidewalk, thanks to the WPA. My brother's friend, Richard Wilcox, tried to burn it, and caught himself on fire. Bill ran toward him yelling and screaming, and the grown-ups came out, and attended to Richard. He was a very sick boy for a while. It left a large scar on his leg.

Bill, not to be outdone, grabbed the back bumper of Dad's car, and held on to it as Dad started driving down the gravel road in front of our house. His feet went up in the air, as he hung on like Superman, and bobbed up and down on the gravel. I went running after them, yelling as loud as I could. Dad was very aggravated, and almost backed up to punish me. Luckily, I was running fast enough to catch up with them by the time he had stopped. Dad saw the scene, and picked Bill up, and took him to the doctor. Bill came home with bandages all over him.

Bill and Richard experienced other troubles from time to time. They chewed coal tar like chewing gum. The net effect was they became black from head to toe with tar even in their hair. They dropped bird eggs from the maple tree on their friends. On one occasion, they stomped some bees from a swarm behind the house, and were stung numerous times before they reached safety.

Life went on. Dad bought us a bull terrier pup. We named him Mickey. He was so little when he arrived that he couldn't even get up on the sidewalk. Mickey yelped the first night, but gradually settled down, and became one of the family. As he got older, a genuine love developed with the family, particularly

Harvey, Bill, and Mickey

between him and my brother. In the picture, we are at Big Springs State Park.

Mickey developed into a first class possum dog, and could catch them wherever they hid. In one case, we heard him barking, and found him underground with honeysuckle vines shaking above him. When we dug him out, we found him retrieving a opossum. The possums would sull, and play dead when confronted. I had watched Dad pick the possums up by the tail, and soon found myself doing the same.

Along with a friend who lived up the street, I decided to create a zoo. The toilet in back of his house smelled so bad that we almost had to find a different yard to set it up. We were forced to place the zoo a safe distance away in far front corner of the lot. We put the possums in two large cardboard boxes next to the sidewalk. The capture, transfer, and caging was a tiring project, and we slept well that night. We dreamed of adding to the zoo population, and expanding. We might even start charging for people to visit it.

The next morning, we were surprised to find large holes in all the boxes, and the possums were gone. Later we learned that the possums in their escape had stopped by the chicken house and bitten the leg off the prime big rooster. The rooster never did crow as loud in the mornings as it had done before.

Our postman, Brother Nanny, was a member of our church. One time, we put Mickey in the mailbox as we saw Brother Nanny coming down the street. When he opened the box, our pup walked out, stood on the door, and looked at him. Needless to say, this made a lasting impression on our postman.

Mickey's second love after possums was cats. Aunt Ina Shell had several of them that lived on and under the back porch. When we went to visit Grandpa Shell, Mickey would start running as we entered the yard, and would propel himself onto the back porch. Cats would go in all directions. It was good training for them. I don't know of a single cat ever being caught by my dog.

Living in the War Years

One has to study war formally in order to survive, and I chose the library as my source for study. A series of books about "Dave Dawson" by Sidney Bowen, were very appealing to me. The character in the book was young, and fought all kinds of battles, winning glorious victories. Dave Dawson was a young American who lived in London when the war began, and was a good friend of a young Englishman. They endured the blitz, and learned about every aspect of warfare. I remember "Dave Dawson at Dunkirk," and "Dave Dawson in the RAF," as especially good books.

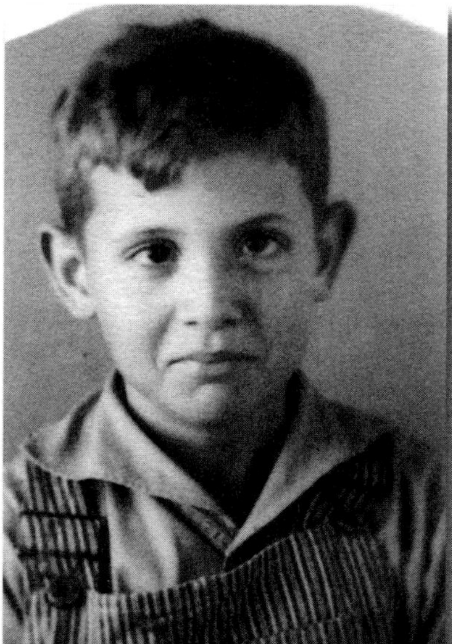

General Harvey Shell

This training seasoned me, and I was ready for War. The picture at left is of a soldier, 10 years old in 1943, and qualified to do battle.

My first battle happened very soon. Dave Dawson had instructed me that one did not throw a hand grenade. It must be lobbed to get the most distance and accuracy out of it. I was at my Mom Wright's farm, and the ground was white with chickens that were feeding. My imagination went wild. I could not see the large flock of chickens, but only an army of men. I slowly picked up a green walnut, and cradled it in my hand. I drew back, and lobbed the hand grenade into the air. While in motion, I yelled "enemy die." The walnut landed in the middle, and the enemy soldiers scattered in all directions – that is all, except one. One wounded soldier lay on the ground. I went into the house, and told Mom Wright that one of her chickens was acting funny. She went back outside with me, and glanced at the chicken. She picked it up and "ranged its neck." There was no more funny chicken, but one that was sent immediately to the fried chicken skillet phase of its act. I never did tell Mom Wright the details of what I had done.

The Army Air Base at Malden suddenly started training pilots. They would fly to Dexter, land, and return to Malden. It went on all day, every day. There were airplanes everywhere, a great contrast to the situation before the War, when would only barely see one or two a day. Experienced pilots also joined in. One pilot flew a P-47 upside down at top speed over the Malden Air Field. He created a lot of attention from both the civilian and army personnel.

My mother was working at Malden, packing parachutes. Sometimes there were crashes, and parachutes would be returned for cleaning and folding. We knew all about parachutes from the newsreels, and the instruction in the Dave Dawson books.

We thought it was easy to build a parachute. One made a simple transition from the peacetime flying of kites to a wartime state of mind. We could tie strings to each of the four corners of a newspaper and be ready for business. We probably jumped off the top of the garage at least a hundred times. However, our chutes did not break the impact of the fall very much. After a time, we gave up the parachutes. We were skinned and bruised all over.

I went into airplane production. I would nail a flat board wing at a right angle across the top of a two-by-four-inch fuselage. Then, I placed a nail in the side to support the body of the plane. I flew the plane, holding on to the wing with the left hand, and the nail with the right. The airplane noise was made by the pilot. Since there were several pilots, several planes were built. My father never asked what was happening to his lumber.

I had a goggle cap. All the boys had them. It was the same type that the pilots wore with flaps over the ears, and goggles at the top.

I wore mine all of the time even when it was warm. It was my hope that someone would come by and enlist me to help fight.

I could name all of the airplane models, both American and enemy. We built a tree house in one of the taller trees in the back, and spied on the airport with binoculars. First, we watched the training planes. When gliders were added to the mix, our project became more interesting. They were pulled by C-47 airplanes, and sometimes there were two gliders hooked to the same plane. They were released from the airplane, and landed at the airport. Later, their tow-line was mounted on two poles in a loop. The airplanes would swoop down, hook them, and they were airborne again. This glider training was for the D-Day Normandy invasion that would occur in Europe.

Convoys came through, and troops pitched tents and camped at the airport while in transit. One time, pup tents were pitched as far as I could see at the airport, and it had rained. The tents were floating. Tanks, jeeps, and guns passed through town on the trains, and there were a lot of them. Soldiers in army trucks passed by our house on the way to load gravel. One of them stopped, and a soldier asked the way to the gravel pit. I volunteered to guide them to it, and climbed into the truck. The soldiers were a couple of kids in uniform, and we enjoyed talking to each other very much. I felt like I was true soldier as I sat with them.

Most of the soldiers smoked factory rolled cigarettes. That was a change from before the war when people carried their tobacco in small bags, and had cigarette papers. They would roll the cigarettes, and lick the paper to complete them before smoking. I was 11 years old, and felt like I should be old enough to smoke like them. I found a new cigarette already rolled. I went behind the house, and into the chicken house. We no longer raised chickens or hogs. I lit the cigarette, and took a large puff. It was good. I continued smoking, inhaling, and enjoying every minute. Then the floor of the chicken house began raising up. I thought that this was strange, but fun. It tilted so much that my nose almost touched it, and I could hardly stand up. Then it crashed down, and I have never been sicker in my life. Smoking could wait for another time.

Other diversions occupied my time. Cecil Wiseman and Eugene Shell, my original cowboy-playing cousins, got a bunch of us together in a nearby storage shed, and made some of the best potato soup I have ever eaten. All of the boys made contributions of onions, potatoes, flour and milk from their homes. The work must have made us hungry. It was good Army chow.

The cousins also supplied me with paw-paws from trees east of Dexter. They were nice yellow fruits about the size of giant cucumbers. They tasted sweet, a little like bananas, but more tart. I loved them, and could never get enough to satisfy my appetite. DeSoto was the first to discover paw-paws, as he searched for the fountain of youth.

We also joined them in eating persimmons. We ate them by the bushel. I had been told that if you cracked open the seeds, small knives, forks, and spoons could be found. I never did find any.

As my cousins grew older with other interests in mind, I was left alone as the commanding officer of my group. My brother Bill, Jimmy Baker, Leon and Buddy Corlew, and Dick Wilcox were in my army. Anyone who happened by was immediately enlisted. Ronald Mouser was a frequent visitor. My allowance had increased, and I purchased five toy pistols in Poplar Bluff for the army – much to my father's surprise. My army spent days building the Burma Road. We dug up all the land across the street, built a cave, and spread the dirt over a wide area.

Our bicycles were absolute necessities. We rode them everywhere in our goggle caps, and would peel off like airplanes into the adjacent yards. The bicycles augmented the wooden planes we had built to make a magnificent Air Corps. One of our favorite actions was to ride up to the beacon-light at the back of the cemetery. We would climb up to the first landing and spy on the Dexter Airport. This was also another chance to check out the hobo camp further down the hill.

There were all types of army things to keep our interest high. Our parents and the newsreels kept us informed about wartime activities such as the Normandy invasion. We had German prisoners of war at the Dexter Airport. They were confined within a fence most of the time. This inspired us, and made the war more realistic in our eyes. The prisoners were glad that the war was over for them, and were happy when they were loaned to farmers for outside work (with guards of course). They were billeted there until the war in Europe was over.

My cousin Cecil was drafted into the army near the war's end, and was shipped to the Philippines. He regularly wrote letters back to his mother, detailing his activities. In one letter, he informed her that he was in a banana-eating contest. To a person who had never had enough bananas to eat, I envied him. He would give the number of bananas that he had eaten so far in each letter. Aunt Alta was getting more and more worried about him as the number increased, and shared her thoughts with the family. I was becoming more envious. The letters stopped. Cecil had developed appendicitis, and had an operation. The contest was over for him. It still sounded like a great contest to me.

My hunger for bananas was increased many fold by Cecil's Stories. I went uptown to Ike Smith's Grocery. He asked me what I needed. I said, "Do you have no bananas?" He said, "Yes, we have no bananas."

Rationing of Commodities

Nearly everything was rationed during the war, including gasoline, tires, shoes, sugar, and other commodities. Private automobiles were no longer being built. We had a 1939 Ford at the beginning of the war, and used it until 1946 when new models became available. I suffered most from the shortage of sugar. Mother made multiple pies and cakes daily, and suddenly the number of them was cut short. White corn syrup was substituted, but did not do the trick. It could be used to make pickled peaches, and to mix with peanut butter for breakfast. We continued to have our gardens, and old ways of preserving food. We had pork, and chicken, and lots of cornbread, beans, butter, eggs and milk.

Mother and Dad took jobs at the Malden Army Air Base in 1943, along with many people from Dexter, including my Uncle Neal Mouser and Charles Wright.

Mrs. Tucker was employed by Mom and Dad to take care of Bill and me while they were away. She kept house and did the ironing. We had an electric fan to make the housework bearable. Mrs. Tucker had trouble getting us to eat the kind of food she felt was nutritious. We wanted only peanut butter and syrup for breakfast, and that was every day. She said, "It won't stick to your ribs." I judged that she didn't know what she was talking about. Nothing was stickier than peanut butter and syrup. My brother did not try to rationalize it. He just liked to eat, and continued to consume it with amazing gusto.

The greatest problem in the rationing program was keeping Bill in shoes. He waded water, and even his new shoes were in shambles a few days after being purchased. Dad ranted and raved about this, and used up all of our ration stamps, as well as those of our grandparents in a very short time. Bill didn't purposely wade water. He just naturally migrated toward it. Finally, Dad bought us some knee-high overshoes. I loved them. We were up at Grandpa Wright's farm when there was an ice storm. We were excited, and put on our overshoes without eating breakfast. We walked out into the field west of the house, and crushed the ice-covered grass with our boots. We ran as fast as we could across the slick field, until we could go no further. We could have been a couple of young tromping mules. Breakfast tasted real good after the long walk back.

The overshoes solved most of the problem. However, there were exceptions. We were on our way to school one morning. The Dexter Creek was up above the normal step stones, and was roaring past. Bill was wearing his overshoes, and I had left mine at home. The solution was simple. Bill could carry me on his back across the creek. I did not have to argue with him. I simply suggested it, and he jumped at the chance. As he waded, water was not only above his overshoes, but soaked his pants up to his crotch. My shoes were slightly splattered, and were pretty much dry. Mark this up for good experience for Bill.

My cousin, Clinton Shell, had been in the garage business in Dexter prior to the War. He traded cars and motorcycles, and made repairs to them when they broke down. He also sold Shetland ponies. When the War began, the sale of new cars ended. This meant multiple repairs for the old cars, and more business for him until the end of the War. He obtained a new Ford Agency when the War ended.

War Savings Bonds were sold throughout the War, and marketed on signs, in movie newsreels, and at work. On the following page is an example of one purchased by Dottie Shell when she worked at the Malden Air Base.

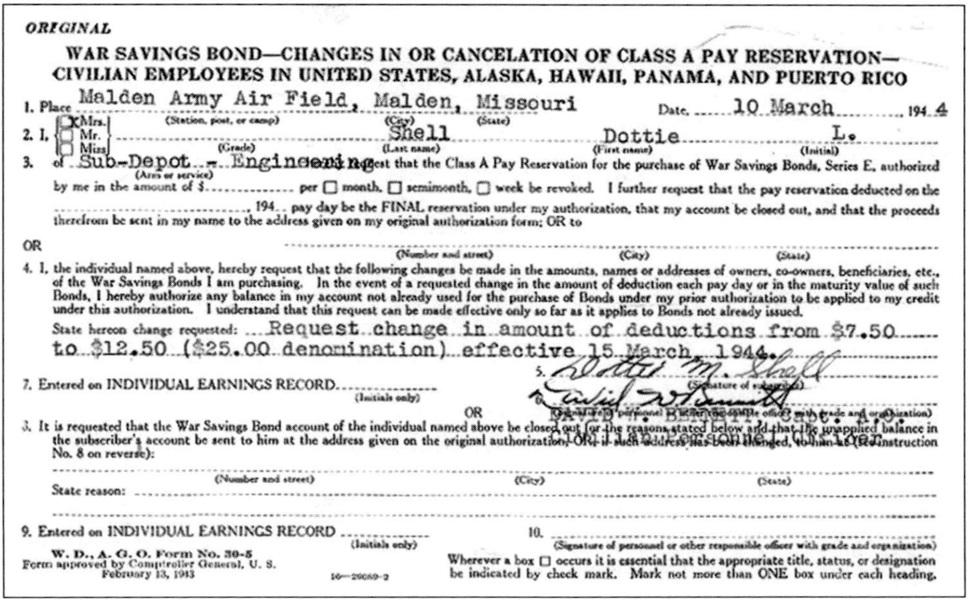

ORIGINAL

WAR SAVINGS BOND—CHANGES IN OR CANCELATION OF CLASS A PAY RESERVATION—CIVILIAN EMPLOYEES IN UNITED STATES, ALASKA, HAWAII, PANAMA, AND PUERTO RICO

1. Place Malden Army Air Field, Malden, Missouri (Station, post, or camp) (City) (State) Date 10 March 1944

2. I, [X] Mrs. [ ] Mr. [ ] Miss (Grade) Shell (Last name) Dottie (First name) L. (Initial)

3. of Sub-Depot - Engineering (Arm or service) request that the Class A Pay Reservation for the purchase of War Savings Bonds, Series E, authorized by me in the amount of $............ per [ ] month, [ ] semimonth, [ ] week be revoked. I further request that the pay reservation deducted on the ...., 194.. pay day be the FINAL reservation under my authorization, that my account be closed out, and that the proceeds therefrom be sent in my name to the address given on my original authorization form; OR to

OR .... (Number and street) (City) (State)

4. I, the individual named above, hereby request that the following changes be made in the amounts, names or addresses of owners, co-owners, beneficiaries, etc., of the War Savings Bonds I am purchasing. In the event of a requested change in the amount of deduction each pay day or in the maturity value of such Bonds, I hereby authorize any balance in my account not already used for the purchase of Bonds under my prior authorization to be applied to my credit under this authorization. I understand that this request can be made effective only so far as it applies to Bonds not already issued.

State hereon change requested: Request change in amount of deductions from $7.50 to $12.50 ($25.00 denomination) effective 15 March, 1944.

5. Dottie M. Shell (Signature of subscriber)

6. David W. Bennett (Signature of personnel or other responsible officer with grade and organization)

7. Entered on INDIVIDUAL EARNINGS RECORD .... (Initials only)

OR

8. It is requested that the War Savings Bond account of the individual named above be closed out for the reasons stated below and that the unapplied balance in the subscriber's account be sent to him at the address given on the original authorization, OR, if such address has been changed, to him at (See instruction No. 8 on reverse):

.... (Number and street) (City) (State)

State reason: ....

9. Entered on INDIVIDUAL EARNINGS RECORD .... (Initials only)

10. .... (Signature of personnel or other responsible officer with grade and organization)

W. D., A. G. O. Form No. 30-5
Form approved by Comptroller General, U. S.
February 13, 1943

16—20080-2

Wherever a box [ ] occurs it is essential that the appropriate title, status, or designation be indicated by check mark. Mark not more than ONE box under each heading.

War Bond

World War II Ends 1945

In 1945, the war continued to drag on. Railroad flat cars still continued to pass through Dexter with tanks and big guns, and the airport was busy with planes and activity. People were weary of the war, and missed and worried about their friends and loved ones. Gold and Silver stars continued to be added to windows around town. Everyone was affected.

Our horizons expanded, and we began to know more about other people, and learn that St. Louis was not in a foreign country. For non-military workers, Southeast Missouri defense plants such as the Malden Air Base provided employment. Others moved to St. Louis, Michigan, and other industrial areas. Victory gardens were planted, particularly by those in Dexter who didn't regularly plant gardens. My mother bought bonds monthly while she worked at the Air Base. We collected and bundled newspapers for war salvage. The government always wanted scrap steel, and some businesses and farmers donated.

I marked my 12th birthday on April 4, 1945. My life somehow was different. I noticed the temperature more, even though the windows at night were open. I would wake up in a sweat, and felt like I was going to smother. One night, a man with a dumpy hat looked in my window. I was up, and had just come in from the back porch. I was scared, and crawled into Dad's bedroom to tell him. He flipped open the back door's wooden toggle, and wandered into the back yard. He could find no one anywhere around. His only weapon was a ball bat, and I was amazed at his courage.

On April 12th, President Roosevelt died. The nation was stunned. He had been crippled by polio throughout his presidency, and his health deteriorated. We knew what polio was. There was not a vaccine for it, and it was continuing to infect people in 1945. Vice-President Truman of Missouri became president. The nation mourned. Many who had almost worshipped Roosevelt felt the nation was lost. The war couldn't be won without him. Well, life went on with President Truman. My father, having been one of the strongest Republicans in Southeast Missouri did not suffer too much with either of them.

Sometime later, I saw my second ghost. That time, we were spending the night at my Aunt Dora Lackey's house. I had slept with the window open. After awhile, something awakened me. The moonlight was shining through a window blind. I looked up, and saw Roosevelt sitting and staring at me. His shadowed face was like a full sized picture pasted on the blind. It was demon-like, and he was smiling. He was looking straight at me!! I closed my eyes, but when I opened them, there he was again. I turned on the light, and he was gone. Much later, I went back to sleep. However, I still claimed the Republicans as my political preference.

School was finally out, and I was ready for a great summer. My father had learned that art treasures recovered from the Nazis were on display in St. Louis. On May 8, 1945, we visited the art museum. We drove up Highway 25, which was paved. At that time, it was completed from Dexter to Aquilla. Then we took gravel roads from Aquilla, and traveled a higher road through Gravel Hill to Advance. From there to Cape Girardeau, alternate sides of the road were paved. So one switched from paved lane to paved lane, pulling over to avoid oncoming traffic. It was smooth sailing from Cape Girardeau to St. Louis on Highway 61.

The art was overwhelming even to a young person like me. There was suddenly excitement in the museum. Someone announced that the war in Europe had ended. We picked up a newspaper after we left, and saw the headlines that VE Day had occurred. That was good news, but the war in the Pacific was still going on, and it was brutal. Boys were still landing on the island beaches, and many were dying.

I awakened on June 18, 1945, and it was an ordinary day. We were finishing breakfast, starting to plan our activities. Suddenly, there was a knock at the door, and my dad answered it. Aunt Dora Lackey entered with panic on her face. "Pop has had another heart attack, and is lying on the ground. I think that he may be dying. He was out by the woodpile when he collapsed." I was numb. This could not be. Dad left with Aunt Dora, and later returned to confirm our worst fears.

I was close to Grandpa Shell. He gave me a lot of attention, and I had learned much from him. I had not been confronted with a loss of such magnitude before. It was the first of many other losses that I would endure during my life.

His casket was placed in the front room of his home, and people could view him there. He was so pale and still. He was not the same person that I had known. It was customary at that time for someone to sit with the dead for 24-hours each day, probably stemming back to the pioneer days or earlier. Finally, a General Baptist minister from Bollinger County came down and preached the funeral. It was held at the Nazarene Church in the Cotton Belt. People from all over the country gathered in, and there was a multitude of flowers. He was placed in a grave in the Dexter Cemetery, about a half-mile north of his home on Crowley's Ridge.

Grandma Shell took the loss very deeply, but having the family around helped a lot, especially being with her two daughters who lived with her. Her sister Amanda (Myers) Shell came to visit her, and they told stories about when they were children. In one case, they had waded the creek in their shoes, and got a spanking. They shared the stories, and laughed and laughed. I couldn't fathom how two women so old could have ever been that young.

Aunt Amanda "Mandie" told a story about an out-body-experience which she had the previous year. She was very sick, and had "died." She visited Heaven, and saw her dad, mother and all of her deceased relatives, and friends. The streets were gold, and there were streams of clear, crystal water. She then returned to life. She told the story with such vigor and conviction, and everyone listened with awe.

Later that year, Grandma Shell developed breast cancer. On November 5, 1945, she joined Grandpa, and lies next to him in a grave on Crowley's Ridge. Her casket was also placed in the front room of the home, and mourners from a wide area attended the funeral.

These losses impacted us greatly. We had been in contact with Grandpa and Grandma Shell almost daily and now it was over. The house was sold, and Aunt Ina and Aunt Dora moved into the house next door to the south.

Below is a picture of some of the family members in the front yard of Aunt Dora' house. At the extreme right of the picture, the Old Bloomfield Road leaves Thrower Street and turns down hill to the west.

Back row from left: Harvey Shell, Dottie Shell, Ina Shell, Neal Mouser, Alta Wiseman, and Dora Lackey. Front row: Minnie Mouser, Neva Mouser.

The summer dragged on, and the war continued. We were hearing stories about the American boys being tortured, and about how tough the invasion of Japan was going to be.

We were in for a big surprise. On August 6, 1945, it was announced that WORLD WAR II HAD ENDED. Victory over Japan, VJ day, had finally been achieved. There would be no invasion of Japan.

I have never experienced such a celebration. Everyone went to town, yelled, shot firecrackers, honked their car horns, and rejoiced until late into the night. Preacher Pounds yelled, threw his hat on the ground, and jumped up and down on it. The families and neighbors gathered, and talked. The excitement continued for weeks.

Americans were not concerned that it took two atomic bombs to end it. The Japanese leaders, Prime Minister Tojo, and Emperor Hirohito would not surrender after the first bomb, even though about 60,000 people had been killed. The second bomb did it.

The War was over! The War was over! The Americans were just relieved to finally have peace. Husbands, brothers, sons, and others would soon be returning. The food rationing would end, and people could finally return to normal. Break out the fatted calf, feast, celebrate, and make new plans.

Our boys started coming home, a few at a time, and then in multitudes. They took jobs, and started business, and everyone started catching up on those things that had been missed during the war. We had a telephone installed. We bought a washing machine, a refrigerator, and a bottle gas stove. Mother had previously used a rubbing-board (washboard), an icebox, and an oil stove.

Dad installed a sewer line and connected water to the house, and we used toilet tissue rather than the sales catalogues that we had used for our outdoor toilet.

Dad dug the sewer trench for the sewer pipe by hand. He then joined the sewer sections together by first pressing asbestos into the female end of the joint, and then pouring molten lead on top of it. The male end of the joint was then pressed in to form a seal. We had other exposures to lead. Our house was painted with lead based paint, as was every house I had ever lived in. We had made lead soldiers, and white lead oxide fumes came off the heater before we poured lead into the molds. We sprinkled arsenic of lead powder on potato plants, and watched dead potato bugs fall off. To my knowledge the lead, asbestos and arsenic never affected our health.

After the War

Dexter thrived after the war as the military returned. The Nelson Addition in the western part of the Cotton Belt Area was expanded, and houses north of the original Highway 60 in uptown Dexter were built. A new subdivision called Hickory Hills was begun further northwest. Such additions created jobs, even for people like me. My enterprising cousin, Ronald Mouser, gave me a job as "substitute newspaper carrier" to deliver in the Nelson Addition.

We rode our bicycles, and I followed Ronald. I didn't know the route, and didn't really learn it during the entire duration of the job. I also had a problem with throwing the paper onto the front step. Many times, it landed on the roof of the house.

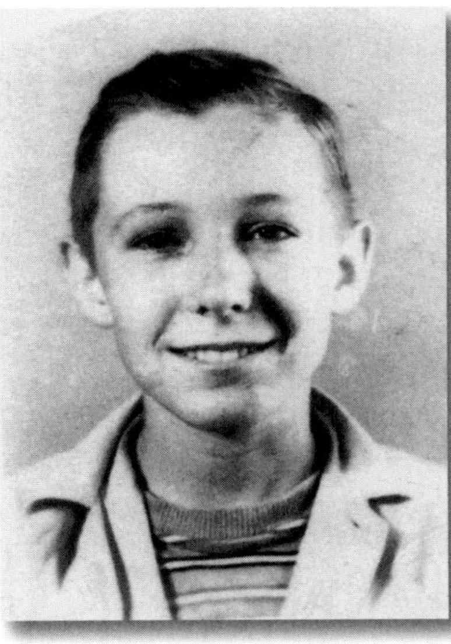

Ronald Mouser

On one trip, a little yellow duck ran out onto the sidewalk and under Ronald's bike. I yelled, "Watch out" but I was too late. His back wheel ran over the duck, and mashed it flat. Much to my surprise, it got up, inflated to its original size, and ran off. I have since learned that when it looks like you are completely down, you can recover to the amazement of all.

Ronald took a position with Parker's drug store as a soda jerk, and I lost my job. I did continue to see Ronald very often, particularly at the soda fountain. We were in the same class at school. We visited back and forth at each others home, and he also spent time with other relatives on Crowley's Ridge. He was very much impressed by my mother's insistence of always baking more that one pie at a time. You always had a choice between at least two kinds.

Mother and Dad quit their jobs at the Malden Air Base. It was nice to have Mother back home. Life was better, and it was nice to have someone at home at the end of the school day. Mom was attentive to community activities, and visited those who were sick. On one occasion, she visited this old man who was very sick and almost dead. The house was hot with summer heat. Bill and I stayed outside and loafed around. There was nothing to do. The grape vines were loaded with green grapes, and we started pulling grapes and throwing them at each other. This later was expanded, and we started throwing them over the house, which had a corrugated tin roof. This made a nice sound, and added an effect to our activity. All of a sudden, Mother burst from the house with the look of total anger on her face. She admonished Bill and me to stop immediately, and we assured her that we would. After she was inside for awhile, the boredom again took its toll, and the activity was repeated. The noise had to be enjoyed by all who heard them. The grapes would go bumpity, bump, bump-bump-bump, as they bounced down the tin roof. Suddenly, mother burst from the house, and herded us up to the car. She picked up a narrow board on the way, and whopped Bill two or three times on the rear. Then she grabbed me, and my first thoughts were you are not going to spank me. I am twelve years old. I put my hand on my rear, and she slapped the board across my fingers. I yelled out in pain, and she was mortified. She had not intended to hurt us. She was forever sorry, but I deserved it. I never did throw grapes again.

Dad took a job with the Sikeston Airport in the salvage department. All of the World War II surplus material had to be salvaged or sold. The effort was repeated by others throughout the country. I remember seeing small ships in the San Diego Harbor that stretched across the water as far as I could see, awaiting disposal.

My appetite for books took on a dimension too great to be satisfied. I read all the time. I started living out the stories in my thoughts. The James Oliver Curwood books caused me to want to live in the wilderness of the North, and to subsist from hunting. My "Grand Ole Opry" ambitions melted away, and were replaced by a dog team. I planned to build a log house next to hot springs for heat. What an improvement. We were still burning coal and wood for heat in Dexter.

The Tom Sawyer and Huckleberry Finn books impressed me the most. I read them multiple times, and even memorized parts of them. I had learned to swim several years earlier, and believed that I could swim the Mississippi River like them, if ever given a chance.

The Dexter Creek was a fair substitute. There were holes in it deep enough to swim, but just barely. Junior Churchill from next door and I decided to cool off at the creek. It was a hot summer day. As usual, we left our clothes on the bank and went skinny dipping. We were sitting in the water up to our necks with everything else hidden. Life was treating us well. We were keeping cool.

Suddenly, Junior's female cousins showed up at our secret place, and demanded that we come out of the water. We howled for them to get away from here. Junior said, "Renee, I am going to tell Grandma, and you are going to get into a lot of trouble." They kept up their demands. All that I could do was groan with embarrassment. Finally, they tired of the adventure, and pulled our clothes on over theirs, and left. That put us into a heck of a situation. We were going to have to slip home naked. Maybe we would have to wait until dark. After a long wait, we got out of the water, and headed down the creek. We of course kept our eyes peeled for the girls, but they had disappeared. We found our clothes nearby which had been discarded, and quickly put them on. We never did know whether the girls had remained and were spying on us. Nor did I know whether Junior had told on them. Tom Sawyer had never had that kind of trouble.

The albatross had fallen from my neck in the sixth grade, and I felt free to live as I pleased.

I was not through with my troubles at the Dexter Creek. I did some deep thinking, and after school started that Fall, I made a plan to play hookey from school, as Tom Sawyer had done. Two of my friends, Paul Montgomery and Charles Rainey, joined me. We went to school in the morning as usual. When the bell rang, we left the school ground, and headed for the creek. We had our lunches with us. We spent the entire day roaming the woods, swimming, and building a hideout. We returned to the school in the afternoon, and joined our friends to go home. No one suspected anything.

The second day was better than the first. We ranged farther, and had a great day. However, my brother and Coreene Sitton walked home with me. She asked me where I was today. I said, "In school as usual." She said, "No you weren't." I said, "You just didn't see me." My brother joined me in my denial. He said, "Yes Harvey was in school today. I came to school with him." Well things went from bad to worse, and before long, it was apparent that I was lying. Bill beat me to the door at home, and immediately told Mother that I had played hookey. She questioned me extensively, and told me that Dad would attend to me when he got home. After an eternity, Dad arrived home, and much to my surprise, he did not spank me. He was very stern. He told me that I would have to confess my sin to my school principal the next day.

I hung around the principal's office, and made as many attempts as I could to muster up the courage to tell him. Nothing happened, and I decided the next day would do just fine. I never could tell the principal. After a few days, Dad asked me if had told the principal. I said, "YES, YES I DID." He asked me what the principal said. I said that he told me not to do it again. Such big lies, and I never told Dad anything different. THOSE WORDS WERE SECURELY STORED UNDER THE BLACK VEIL THAT I WORE.

I was still looking for a way to make a living. I decided to try boxing. A good boxer could make a lot of money. A group in Dexter was sponsoring the golden gloves. I had read about how it was done, and felt like I could succeed at it.

We bought a set of gloves, and invited everyone on our street of our size to attend our boxing match. I had a prime boxer that

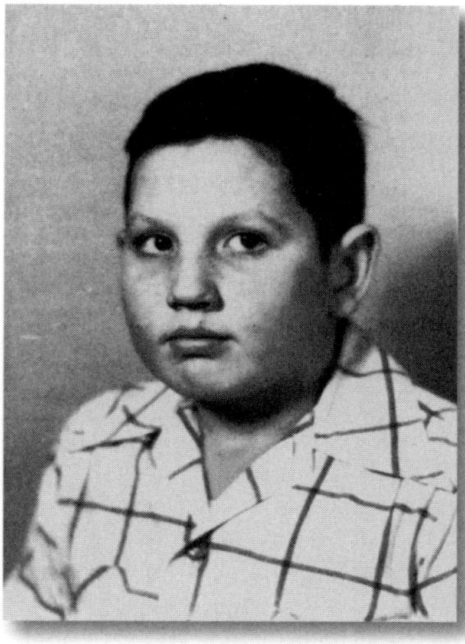

Bill Shell

I would use first on all the participants, and then I would then finish him off, and become the champion. He was my brother, Bill.

You can see how tough he was in the picture.

The boxing event took place in the driveway, south of the house. There were ripe blue plum trees along the side, and The Maple on the hill was to the west. We put on the gloves and whammed away. Those not fighting ate blue plums. Bill fought every bout. However, I was not pleased with the way that he fought. Instead of holding up his guard, and dancing around like a normal boxer, he just swung his arms around like a pile driver, one-over-the-other, and advanced to the front. Probably by the time everyone had been beaten by Bill, we had eaten 1,000 plums. It was my turn, and the gloves were on. I put my guard up, and crouched, as I danced toward him. His arms spun around, and he knocked my guard down each time I approached him. The outcome was that I was totally defeated by that primitive style of fighting of my brother. My career of boxing ended before I hardly got started. The Maple Tree smiled.

We fished and hunted at every opportunity. Dad had bought me a .410 gauge shotgun, and taught me how to use it. A lot of our fishing was done in the St. Francis River. The Wappapello Dam had been completed in 1941 to control flooding along the St. Francis. The river was still wild with woods lining it on both sides. The land along it was not drained, and much of it was swampy. It was believed that panthers still lived on it, and attacked the livestock from time to time. We pole fished for carp with my cousin, Cecil Wiseman and his family. The carp were caught as fast as we could drag them in. The family then canned them to eat at a later date.

On one trip with my father and brother, our luck was not with us. We were fishing with live bait to try to lure some catfish, but we caught nothing. On our way home, we stopped at a camp owned by a friend from Dexter, Bill Phillips. Several other people had also stopped by. He had some large catfish, and in a short time, they were frying in lard. We sat down to eat fried potatoes, cornbread, onions, and fish. Black coffee, boiled in a pot, was added. It was one of the best meals that I ever had.

The Lamentations of the Maple

In 1947, my dad moved the family to the Missouri Ozarks. We were leaving to never reside again on Crowley's Ridge. The Maple was weeping. Our grandparents no longer lived there, and business opportunities were pulling people away to all parts of the country.

Dad had started a new automobile business, and obtained the Ford Motor Company franchise in Ellington, Missouri. Clinton Shell had the franchise in Dexter.

People had been without new cars for a long time, and were desperate to obtain them. A waiting list was kept, and the cars were sold in the order of sign-up. The prices were controlled by the government, and agency called the "Operation of Price Administration (OPA)." Otherwise, prices would have gone out of sight. This put the dealers under a lot of pressure, because people were demanding new cars immediately. We could have placed any price we wanted, and could have gotten it, except for the OPA regulations.

Dad allowed trade-ins on the new cars, and on one occasion, a 1934 Ford was the only car we had left. We went for a drive out through the countryside. The floor in the back had holes in it. We started to cross a creek, and my brother and I were excited. We could look through the holes, and see the water. Suddenly to our surprise, the water started squirting up through the holes like little fountains, and the car settled to the bottom of the creek and stopped. It would not start. We raised our feet into the seats to keep them dry. Dad, Bill, and I rolled down the windows. We climbed onto the top of the car, and crawled to the end where we could jump onto the bank. Mother was abandoned in the car, and could not make the exit. We found a farmer with some mules who came down and pulled us out. Everyone, including Mother, was very happy. However, Dad did not ever trade down again to cars as old as that one.

The picture below shows Clinton Shell and my Father at a Ford truck meeting in Detroit. They rode a bus to the meeting, and drove new trucks back. The entertainment for the night was a dinner in one of the Chase Hotel meeting rooms, and Dina Shore sang for the group. Dad was very impressed.

Ford Truck Meeting

Clinton is sitting at the extreme left in the picture in the back row, and Dad is sitting in the same row, fifth from left.

The little town of Ellington was unique. When you descended into it from any direction, the integral vista was magnificent. All the elements were pristine. They blended with the landscape colors to complete a pleasant picture. My mother said almost daily, "Oh, it is so beautiful." She had almost forgotten the Maple on the Hill. She changed her theme song to "In the Pines, In the pines, Where the Sun Never Shines, and Oh the Cold winds blow."

There were cattle drives down the main-street with real cowboys. I was still not divorced from my cowboy days, and the drives excited me.

Corrals were located at the end of the street next to our garage. A man, nicknamed "The Judge," was available to estimate the weight of the cattle. He would work for just a few dollars. His estimates were quite accurate, and helped the cowmen to project their earnings for each drive. He was a regular at each cattle drive.

Fistfights were a weekly occurrence on Saturday afternoons behind the drugstore – that is, until a highway patrolman was assigned to that district. Prior to that time, our town marshal, Bulldog, was afraid to intervene. They would take him by the arms and lead him away. He had acquired his nick-name when someone asked him kill a vicious dog. When he arrived at their house, he was told that the dog was down in the field tied to a tree. He approached it, and fired. It was a routine duty that he had carried out many times. That time, things went wrong. He missed the dog, and shot the rope in two. The dog lunged at him. He climbed the tree and the dog sat below and kept him at bay. When the dog would leave, he would climb down, only to be chased up again. He spent the entire afternoon in the field before he was able to escape.

Once the Highway patrolman started visiting him in Ellington, he recovered his bravery. That time, when people would get out of line, he would rake his nightstick across their heads. That brought him a lot of respect, and the City became law abiding. Then people called him by his given name, and Bulldog was forgotten.

Leaving Dexter was a difficult move for me. I lost the security of being surrounded by all my relatives. The pull of the maple was very strong. Soon I adjusted, and found the area to be the most fascinating in the world. I spent summers fishing and swimming in the creek. Throughout the year, I hunted and explored the woods.

I would get up in the mornings before Mom and Dad, and head for the woods. I chased the squirrels with my trusty shotgun and hit one once and awhile.

I also explored caves, although now I don't know how I was so brave. The caves were often a tight fit. Sometimes we had to get down and crawl through narrow parts. Bats sometimes covered the ceilings. Maybe I was just crazy at the time.

Lighting A Lantern for the Cave Adventure
Harvey Steele, Ronnie Taylor, and Harvey Shell
(Ronnie is wearing a goggle cap in the picture.)

Movies on Saturday afternoon were also our favorites in Ellington. They were generally cowboy shows, and the rooms were packed. Electric fans in the back of the theater kept the temperature tolerable. Everyone had boxes of popcorn that they threw when things got exciting, and sometimes things really got exciting. If the film broke or there was a power failure, you couldn't see the seats in front of you for the popcorn boxes that were thrown. Some wrestling took place as well.

During the summer, we were barefooted. It was convenient since we spent most of the time at the creek. The hot dust from the road squished up between our toes, and had a very soothing effect on our moods.

My new shotgun served me well. It was even good for protection. One night, I head voices and saw lights in the back of the house. I told Dad that someone was out there to steal my tame rabbits. I grabbed my shotgun, and headed for the door when Dad grabbed me. Actually, there was a crew out there cleaning our outdoor toilet. If I had fired that shotgun over their heads, no telling what would have happened.

School was fun, and I started to find that the girls were nice, and not to be avoided. There were many outdoor adventures. I wanted to learn to catch fish with my hands ("hog" them). Another friend, Jake Hampton, who was a year younger than Ronnie Taylor and me, claimed that he was very experienced at hogging fish. He gave us advice on hogging fish, as well as other wildlife stories. He told us that disturbing a "Shiagpolk" would result in our being attacked, and having our eyes pecked out. Since then I have discovered that the "Shiagpolk" was a blue heron.

We were walking down Logan Creek one day when the largest bullfrog that ever lived jumped off the bank in front of us. It swam through the clear water, and under a small clump of roots in the middle of the creek. We said "okay Jake, he's yours." Jake agreed but wanted to use the frog gig first. We finally relented, and he walked to the middle of the creek and pushed the gig under the roots. A big snake swam out, and across the creek. Jake killed the snake, and came back to get the frog. We never got the frog, but six snakes came out from under the roots.

I became adept at chasing snakes in the creek, grabbing them by the tail, and throwing them up on the bank.

One time while "hogging" fish with my hands, my friend, Ronnie Taylor and I were caught by the game warden. Ronnie had been gigging. We were told to take the gig home and to tell our fathers about our encounter with the law. Dad was primarily concerned with the dangers of hogging fish, especially about a possible snake bite. He didn't know that I was doing it. I promised him that I would not hog fish anymore. I meant it, and managed to avoid the temptation for about a month. One day when the woods were hot, and we were sweating, my friend and I decided to hit the creek. I remembered my promise, and just enjoyed the cool water. My friend started hogging fish, and he caught several. I ignored him. He suddenly yelled, "Come here Harvey. There is a big bass under my foot. Reach back under the bank, and pull him out." Well, that was too much. I grabbed the bass, pulled him out and started catching all the fish that I could find. My promise to Dad was forgotten, and I was having the time of my life. My stupor was suddenly broken. A big snake swam between my fingers, and I felt his entire length glide through. That was the last time that I hogged fish.

There was a big, yellow bulldog that lived at a house that I passed every day. He was an especially angry dog. When my dog and I passed by, he would come around the house, growl, bark, snarl, and throw himself sideways against the picket fence – almost knocking it down. I learned to enjoy the daily bout, and encouraged my dog to "get'im, get'im." One day the bulldog came around the house with such speed, and force that he jumped the fence, and landed in the middle of us. My dog immediately recovered and charged him. The bulldog was out of his territory, and scared to death. My dog ran him completely off. Since then, I have noticed that people react the same way when out of their territory.

We lived our last year in Ellington in a haunted house. I know this because the Judge told me so. He said the home where we moved was his family homestead. The left side was log (boxed in) and the right side was frame. It was mounted on large stones. He said that an Indian had been killed in the loft of the log part, and that strange events had occurred ever since. I would sneak up there and look around, but I never did see anyone. At the back of the house was a long back porch without doors that reached from one end to the other.

My Mother was strongly convinced that it was haunted. It was located south of town in the country. It was dark when we got home, and spooky. One night, the house was full of gas when we got home. It had leaked from the bottle gas stove. Someone had turned it on. There was a goat that frequently ran all the way across the porch at night, making a loud clattering sound. One night, we heard a clink-clink-clink, clink-clink-clink, and Dad went out to investigate. I felt more at ease to stay in. Mom was scared, and I needed to protect her. At least that is what I told myself. Dad called me outside, and he was laughing. A skunk had its head caught in a mayonnaise jar, and was clinking it against the step. Dad hit the jar lightly with a mop handle, and it broke. The skunk staggered slowly away, and gave us no more trouble.

The house turned out to be a happy place after our fears had subsided. We would sit in front of a large fireplace at night, and read or talk. Sometimes we would make popcorn in the fireplace. Bill learned how to bull-fight the goat, and it learned how to charge him. If he got bored, he would straddle the goat and ride it down the hill.

During 1947, we made a trip to California with the Clinton Shell family. He was my father's nephew, although about the same age, and he liked to drive fast. He equally cherished coffee and cigarettes. One time, when returning from Bloomfield to Dexter, he picked up a hitchhiker who rode in the back seat. Clint drove at his usual wide-open speed, and his passenger was praying before he got to Dexter. He told Clinton never to pick him up again.

Anyway it was a fast trip to California. We drove to Yellowstone and spent the night at the Lodge. At that time, there were wooden bunks, and dusty blankets. We then departed through Colorado, drove over the mountains. In the mountains, we constantly had problems with vapor-locks in our cars. We would just pull over, and let the engines cool, and then start on our way again.

Max Domiguez, Chlo (Harper) Domiguez, and Forest Harper

Las Vegas, Nevada was on our route. It was no big deal. The Strip did not exist at that time. The Golden Nugget Casino and Fremont Hotel were located on a wide street, and the doors were open to the street to make the heat bearable. I was interested in a gambling device that would let you reach for a silver dollar with a grab hook. I don't know whether we tried or not, but probably once or twice. Then it was on to San Diego. The ocean, fisheries, and ships interested me. There was also smog. We visited with Chlo and Max Domiguez who lived there. Max had emigrated from Cuba (before Fidel Castro). He offered to teach me Spanish, but there was not time. Max is standing in front of an avocado tree. Their nephew Forest Harper is standing with them.

We drove back home on the southern route, and it was hot. We did not have air conditioners on our cars, and air coming through the windows felt like a blast furnace. The stop in Yuma for gas was especially hot. We bought a canvas water bottle that we hung outside on the hood ornament. Water would seep through the canvas, evaporate, and cool the water. Our travel then took us through the Salt River Canyon, over the mountains, and to White Sands, New Mexico.

White Sands, New Mexico.
From left: Sue, Phyllis, Harvey, Patsy, and Bill Shell.

White Sands, New Mexico
Back from left: Clifford, Sue, Harvey, Phyllis, and Bill Shell. Front: Patsy Shell

We saw no UFOs in 1947 as we traveled through Roswell, or anything else to take our breath away. However, it was a great trip with my cousins.

There were lots of sights to remember. The Apache Indians had temporary shelters along the road where they sold trinkets, jewelry, and other goods. The sales force was primarily made up of women, and they had their children and babies with them. It was fun to talk to them. The Indian women managed well, although it was hot and dusty. They sold their wares, and nursed their babies between the conversations. The other little children had a great time running and playing.

Indian sales along a road in New Mexico.

The Move Back to Dexter

In 1948, my father sold the business, and we moved back to Dexter. He opened a Studebaker Agency, and built a new building. Note the Studebaker in front.

It was a new dealership, and all new files had to be set up. Since Betty Jo Wright could type, she was hired by Dad to help. She catalogued all the car parts and put them in a file so dad would know just what he had and where to find it. This took several weeks of the summer. Dad could never quite sell Clinton Shell

Shell Motor Company

or my Grandpa Wright on the good qualities of a Studebaker; and they both steadfastly remained Ford men.

The building was located on the east side of Highway 25, across from Clinton Shell's garage. Crowley's Ridge is behind it. However, we did not return to Crowley's Ridge to live, but moved to the Cotton Belt. My interests were changing, and I became addicted to classical music. I would typically spend an entire Sunday afternoon listening to a radio station in St. Louis that broadcast continuous classical music. I continued to read, and spent more time at the soda fountain. I attended about all the football and basketball games.

Everyone at high school had grown taller, and changed dramatically. I did not really know them anymore. Again, I felt insecure, and had to adjust. Nevertheless, high school was fun. I was in the band, glee club, and developed a close friendship with several people. John Gaines and Wayne McMullen were my best friends.

I had never learned to dance at Ellington, and was lost when I attended the high school dances at Dexter. At my first dance, I stood around, and watched the others dancing. Vivian Allen asked me why I didn't dance, and I told her that I didn't know how. She said, "It's easy," and offered to teach me. Although I refused at first, I later agreed, holding her and following her steps. It was easy, and wonderful. I will forever be indebted to Vivian Allen, a classmate since kindergarten. My insecurity in moving to Dexter took a giant step in fading away.

I was also the recognized school artist and cartoonist, along with my friend John Gaines. However, there were no more drawings of nudes. I had learned my lesson. I did draw a recognizable picture of one of our strictest teachers who inspired the fear of God in most of my classmates. I featured her wearing a bikini. This achievement won me the highest praise from my male classmates, and the teacher never knew about it. I don't know what happened to the picture. Maybe I threw it into the weeds. It was one more entry UNDER MY BLACK VEIL.

Highway 25 had not yet been built from Aquilla, Missouri to Advance, Missouri, and a large swamp called Swan Pond was located north of Aquilla. We visited it one day, and got in a boat that could be poled along. After some distance, the swamp got wider and there were lily pads. Suddenly, we started seeing snakes, and then more and more snakes. They were on every lily pad, sometimes in multiple numbers. Dad said, "Maybe it's time to get out of here." Bill and I readily agreed. As Dad poled the boat along, some of the snakes started following. The number increased to four or five abreast, swimming as fast as they could. Dad hit at them with the pole, and then pushed us along. I guess that they thought the boat was a log, and had we stopped, they would have joined us in the boat. Dad kept poling the boat along, and after a time we lost them. After we got out near the car, we saw an isolated pond that was alive with fish. Dad got a stick, and raked some of them out. They were large Grinnell fish, weighing at least five or more pounds each. We left them, since they were boney, and not a very good fish to eat.

The Maple Reminisces

Dexter had changed after the war, but we still didn't have air conditioning in our homes or cars. Electric fans were everywhere. They were starting to build farm-to-market roads, and rural electric lines. We had water in most homes, household appliances, better medicine, plentiful food, and new automobiles. However, the families would never need to depend upon each other, or be as close as they were before the war. My brother Bill and I soon parted, and went our separate ways. Bill became a medical doctor and practiced Internal Medicine in Sikeston, Missouri for his entire career. He married Patricia Duggins of Dexter.

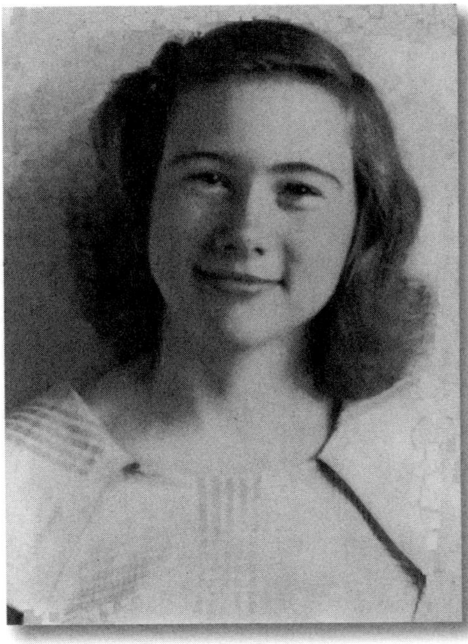

Joanne Bagby

My soul mate, Joanne Bagby had moved to Vinson on a farm. She attended the Dexter High School, and the Vinson Baptist Church. I had not met her yet. I would have to wait a few years before my dream would become a reality.

The journey has been short. The early part of my life crawled at a snail's pace. It speeded up during mid-life, and is racing at present. Certainly, I made some mistakes in the past, but there have been many rewards. I would not hesitate to do it all over again. Like the poet William Wordsworth, "my heart still leaps up when I behold a rainbow in the sky / so it was when my life began / so it was when I was a man / and so it is since I've grown old / And I could wish my remaining days / to be bound each to each by natural piety." Of course, my early life began with views through a goggle cap, and from under a maple tree.

Although I never did return to live on Crowley's Ridge, I cherish my experiences with the people who had lived there. *Goodspeed's History of Southeast Missouri*[14] lists thousands of people who lived and contributed to the Bootheel history, but have been lost to everyone's memory forever. They have all vanished. It did not matter whether they were ordinary persons, beggars, lawyers, judges, doctors, teachers, or elected governmental officials, they vanished. As time has passed, many of my family members have joined them in antiquity. The Ridge itself has changed, and is no longer familiar. Omar Khayyam wrote, "The Moving Finger writes; and, having writ, moves on: nor all thy Piety nor Wit Shall lure it back to cancel half a Line, nor all thy Tears wash out a Word of it." So it was with my life on Crowley's Ridge.

With this in mind, I will close this story with a poem that I wrote when I was seventeen years old. It was inspired by the chimes of my Grandpa Shell's clock:

I watched a time piece wind its way,
Through ages but to me a day,
The drummings deep within it wrought,
A melancholy voiceless thought,

That manifested ceaseless time,
With every beat a soul ground fine.
Beggars, statesmen, kingdoms, thieves,
Their lives are only as the leaves,

They flare out early in the spring,
Bright, joyous, glorious things,
But when the winds of autumn call,
Grow dull dejected in their fall.

For all things have their place and span,
And although high and mighty man,
Lifts up his writings words and deeds,
His time will come for other needs.

For there is the drumming of the clock,
Which willfully will never stop,
But ceaselessly go ringing on,
Forgetting man was ever born.

Epilogue

by Joanne (Bagby) Shell

It was one of the hottest days on record in a farmhouse in Southeastern Missouri that I decided to come into this world. Parma, Missouri, is located just 25 miles from New Madrid, the center of the famous earthquake of the early 1800s.

I probably caused a minor earthquake myself when my mother became pregnant with me. I definitely was not a planned baby. My older brother was only 13 months older than I. Not only did she have two babies to contend with, but also a hired field hand lived at our home. Extra cooking, cleaning, and other work had to be done. She had to boil the water in a big iron kettle, scrub the clothes clean on a big washboard, and hang them outside on a clothesline to dry. Mondays were the washdays. Wood had to be carried in for both cooking and heating the home. There was no indoor plumbing.

While Harvey was growing up on Crowley's Ridge, I was living in the flat low land of the Delta. I had similar experiences to his, even during World War II. One day, school let out for us to go see a glider that had landed on a farm.

Parma was a quiet town much like Dexter. People gathered in on Saturdays to visit and to be entertained. One such event occurred when two ladies from Malden, Missouri came rolling into town in a new Model T. Everyone came out and lined the streets to watch. Unfortunately, the driver had not been taught how to stop the car. The town drunk was the most excited of all, and ran out in the street to view it. He got too close and the car ran over him.

It knocked him down, and kept going. People ran out, and picked him up, and dusted him off. The car kept rolling down the street, and finally circled around and came back. The people were just as excited as they were during the first trip. So was the town drunk. He ran out into the street, and they ran over him a second time. He got up, and watched the ladies proceed out of town with little remorse. He had been able to get a close-up view of the new car.

My parents were young when they were married. My father had a 12th grade education, and my mother had an 8th grade education. Her parents lived too far from the nearest high school for her to attend.

One night after visiting mother, my Dad was walking home along a levee road. There was moonlight, but all he could see was water. It stretched out on each side of the road. He had some distance to go, and was all alone. Suddenly, he heard a dog running toward him. It got closer, and he tried hard to see it. It kept getting closer, and he still couldn't see it. It ran past, and the sound of the footsteps continued as it faded away into the distance behind him. He never did see the dog, but he said that the small hairs on the back of his neck stiffened.

The Bagby Family
Joanne, Birdie, Geneva, Dirl, and Jerry

Mother and Dad both came from farming families, so they naturally became farmers too. When they were first married, they lived a short time with my father's family, and remained there until they could rent and eventually own their own farm.

This was during the Great Depression, and times were hard. It was difficult to scrape up enough money to make payments on the farm.

They worked hard and

were self-sufficient. They had a garden, cows, and chickens. There was plenty of meat, eggs, milk, and butter available, and vegetables from the garden could be canned. We were not hungry during the depression. My father always said that the only way that we knew that a depression was happening was that people started returning from the cities in the North to join us back on the farm.

Three years later, my sister was born, which completed our family. In the meantime, my father had purchased a larger farm. Although my father was a farmer at heart, he never missed the opportunity to pursue that American dream of bigger and better things for his family.

Shortly after my sister was born, we moved again. My father bought a farm implement store in town and sold John Deere farming equipment.

Bagby Implement

I am sitting on the tractor, and my Dad is behind me. Notice the design of the old tractors.

By the time I was five, he sold the store, and bought another farm where I was to grow up, and where I lived until I was married.

I married and took Harvey's name in 1955. I have lived with him for 53 years. Two children and five grandchildren have been born to this union.

References

The references used in the story include the following. Also, credit is given to the relatives and friends who supplied some of the stories and pictures:

1. United States 1895 Atlas, Missouri 1895 Map, Rand-McNally. Copyright www.memoriallibrary.com.

2. *The Shell Family*, David L. Shell, Candor Press, Dexter, Missouri, May 1953. Harvey Shell, Sr., my father edited the book for David Shell, and had it printed.

3. USGS Map, 1934, Bollinger County, Missouri (Map owned by Harvey Shell).

4. Drawing showing Homestead layout (by Harvey Shell).

5. Map, *Trails and Post Roads, A Travel Guide for the Southeast Missouri Region*, Prepared by the SE Missouri Regional Planning and Economic Development Commission.

6. *Shoe Cobbler's Kin,* by Lorena S. Eaker, Baltimore, Gateway Press, 1976, and other publications. All of these books by Lorena S. Eaker are very informative, and represent a great deal of effort. Names and Shell chronological data are well documented.

7. Family notes about the Wright and Harper families by Florance Hyslop Bright and Betty Wright Allen.

8. Map, Missouri 1833 (Map owned by Harvey Shell).

9. USGS Map, 1939, Stoddard County, Missouri (Map owned by Harvey Shell).

10. "The Long Road," Neal Edgar Mouser, a short synopsis of his life, 1978. Submitted by his son Ronald Mouser.

11. Drawing showing Crowley's Ridge area (by Harvey Shell).

12. Lyrics to the "Maple on the Hill" the Carter Family, 1939.

13. *History of Missouri from the Earliest Explorations and Settlements until the Admission of the State into the Union,* by Louis Houck, Chicago: R.R. Donnelley & Sons Co., 1908, 3-volume set (Missouri Historical Society).

14. *Goodspeed's History of Southeast Missouri,* First Printing 1888, Goodspeed Publishing Company, A Reprint Edition 1955 by Ramfre Press, Cape Girardeau (Harvey Shell Library).

About the Author

Harvey D. Shell left high school at the end of his junior year in 1950 with enough units to enter college. He earned a BS degree in chemistry and biology at SEMO State College, Cape Girardeau, Missouri when he was barely 20 years old. He taught science and mathematics for one year at Gray Ridge High School, and was drafted into the U.S. Army.

Harvey D. Shell

After serving in the Army for two years, he obtained a BS Degree in Chemical Engineering from the School of Mines and Metallurgy, Rolla, Missouri. He is a Registered Professional Engineer.

He worked as a Technical Supervisor for Mallinckrodt Chemical Company, Weldon Spring, Missouri in their uranium processing plant for two years. He then joined Pennsalt Chemical Corporation, Calvert City, Kentucky. There he designed equipment in the general engineering department of various types, including a large distillation column. He then supervised the technical startup of a new sodium chlorate plant, and later became the production supervisor of a hydrofluoric/sulfuric acid plant complex.

In 1966, he attended the University of Missouri-Columbia, and worked for one year towards a Master's Degree in Chemical Engineering. A summer job in 1967 developed into full-time employment with the Missouri Air Conservation Commission, the state agency responsible for controlling air pollution in Missouri. He became director of the state agency. He was responsible for hiring the staff, obtaining funds from the appropriations committees, establishing an air monitoring network, meeting with the Commission and public, promulgating the air emission regulations, and coordinating his activities with the EPA. He served on several state and federal committees. He was appointed by Bill Ruckleshause to the National Manpower and Education Committee, and was elected as head of the State and Territorial Air Pollution Program Administrators.

He left the state, and established Shell Engineering & Associates, Inc. in 1975. The firm consults in environmental engineering matters, and is still active after 33 years. Consulting work has been done in virtually all the continental United States. Internationally, it has done work in Labrador, Quebec, Russia, Columbia, Indonesia, China, Oman, Kazakhstan, and Nigeria. Training has been offered with funding from the USAID.

Mr. Shell was born in 1933, and experienced the years of the Great Depression and World War II. He is retired and his son Charles Shell, PE, operates the company. He spends his retirement time writing, producing video material, and pursuing other hobbies.

Index

D

E

N

O

P

R

S

T

U

V

W

Z